W9-BCM-183

ALSO BY IRIS KRASNOW

Surrendering to Motherhood

Surrendering to Marriage

Surrendering to Yourself

I Am My Mother's Daughter

The Secret Lives of Wives

Sex After…

CAMP GIRLS

CAMP GIRLS

Fireside Lessons on Friendship,
Courage, and Loyalty

IRIS KRASNOW

GRAND CENTRAL
PUBLISHING

NEW YORK   BOSTON

Grand Central Publishing
Hachette Book Group
1290 Avenue of the Americas, New York, NY 10104
grandcentralpublishing.com
twitter.com/grandcentralpub

First Edition: April 2020

Grand Central Publishing is a division of Hachette Book Group, Inc. The Grand
Central Publishing name and logo is a trademark of Hachette Book Group, Inc.

The publisher is not responsible for websites (or their content) that are not owned
by the publisher.

The Hachette Speakers Bureau provides a wide range of authors for speaking
events. To find out more, go to www.hachettespeakersbureau.com or call
(866) 376-6591.

All photos courtesy of the author.

Library of Congress Cataloging-in-Publication Data
Names: Krasnow, Iris, author.
Title: Camp girls : fireside lessons on friendship, courage, and loyalty / Iris Krasnow.
Description: First edition. | New York : Grand Central Publishing, 2020. | Summary:
"Iris Krasnow started going to summer camp at age 5. She sat around a fire roasting
marshmallows until they burned; chased fireflies that dotted the night sky; swam in
the expansive Blue Lake; and made friends that have lasted a lifetime, learning
lessons along the way that she follows to this day. Now decades later, she returned to
Camp Agawak in Wisconsin as a staff member to help resurrect Agalog, the camp's
defunct magazine that she wrote for as a child. She's been doing this every summer
for five years, participating in the same activities she loved as a young girl now filled
with the wisdom, perspective, and appreciation that comes with age. A nostalgic,
reminiscent memoir written from the heart, CAMP GIRLS details the essential life
skills that formed who Iris became, and also the feelings of belonging to a family, not
of blood, but of history, loyalty, and tradition. For Iris and many others, camp is key
to fulfillment and success in life"—Provided by publisher.
Identifiers: LCCN 2019041817 | ISBN 9781538732267 (hardcover) |
ISBN 9781538732243 (ebook)
Subjects: LCSH: Camps for girls—Wisconsin. | Camps—Social aspects. | Campers
(Persons)—United States—Biography. | Krasnow, Iris—Childhood and youth.
Classification: LCC GV197.G5 K73 2020 | DDC 796.54/2082--dc23
LC record available at https://lccn.loc.gov/2019041817

ISBNs: 978-1-5387-3226-7 (hardcover), 978-1-5387-3224-3 (ebook)

Printed in the United States of America

LSC-C

10   9   8   7   6   5   4   3   2   1

To Oscar Siegel, for introducing me to
Camp Agawak
To Mary Fried, for bringing me back
To my camp girls, for everything

CAMP GIRLS

Why Camp?

I still go to the summer camp I loved as a child, having returned after a forty-year hiatus to resurrect the camp magazine where I got my literary start at the age of eight. Just like when I was a young camper, leaving at the end of the season is so sad, so hard.

We stay up all night and sob.

Summers long ago, when camp was over and school was starting, I had to wait a whole ten months to return. As a sixty-four-year-old woman with grown children, I can go back to visit any time. Last fall, I was called—yanked really—to do just that.

Several weeks after the official end of the Camp Agawak season, I was longing for the solitude of the woods, to savor the Wisconsin forest without the cacophony of 250 girls. So I traveled for a weekend retreat to the cabin I have inhabited for the past six summers.

I left seventy-two-degree Annapolis for forty-two-degree Minocqua, a journey that took a forty-minute car ride to the airport in Baltimore and a two-hour plane ride to Chicago, where I was picked up by a camp bestie, Liz Weinstein, for a five-hour drive to northern Wisconsin.

We agreed to spend the first morning apart, and I sought out the bench near Blue Lake where I have sat many mornings, over many decades. The docks were down, as were the royal-blue blow-up slide and yellow floating trampoline, toys we did not have in the old days but now are planted on many camp waterfronts.

It was only me and the water and the sky and the memories. There were no screaming campers or loud motorboats.

In an empty camp, my history holder, I was every age.

I saw myself walking slowly out of the lake in our uniform navy-blue Jantzen one-piece swimsuit, cold and exhausted the day I passed the last dive for my advanced yellow cap. I saw myself as the fifteen-year-old captain of the Blue Team, at the stern of the war canoe, beating the White Team boat by a mere two yards.

I saw dozens of tiny boats crafted out of birch bark and ablaze with candles, lolling in the shallow end and set adrift by campers, after we each made a wish the last night of camp.

My wish was always the same: that I would return to Agawak next June, on a bus with my camp girls, chewing Bazooka and singing: "In the Northwoods of Wisconsin, beneath the sky so blue, where the pine trees are above us and the friendships are so true."

I saw that I would travel a thousand miles and a thousand hours just for a glimpse of the shimmer of this lake, to the place where I feel whole and more of everything.

Soon after returning home, I am visiting with Gail Watkins, my next-door neighbor, and she is showing me black-and-white Polaroids of the tent she slept in seventy years ago, at Echo Hill Camp, on Maryland's Chesapeake Bay.

"Some of the happiest times of my life," Gail is saying, misty-eyed, as she sifts through the tattered pages of her photo album, with its peeling green canvas cover and broken spine. The pictures are hardly decipherable, the black now gray, the white a pale yellow.

Yet as she approaches her eightieth birthday, there is nothing faded in her memory as Gail recalls vivid snapshots of the twelve summers spent at Echo Hill, starting at the age of six. She evokes clear scenes of treasure hunts through the woods, with the treasure being trunks filled with Creamsicles, and of her beloved counselor Gracie, who stroked Gail's hair at night as she read the campers bedtime stories.

The creativity spawned in Arts & Crafts helped seed Gail's lengthy career as an acclaimed visual artist who shows her work in galleries world-wide.

Gail hands me a rough mosaic collage, made of triangle cutouts of construction paper, pieced together with Elmer's Glue at camp in 1952. "This is where it all started," she says.

Camp, too, is where it all started for me. I spent my first summer at Camp Agawak for Girls in 1963, which would turn into ten summers as a camper and counselor. All that is very adventurous, very sentimental, very brave, and very naughty about who I am today was birthed and nurtured there.

My Polaroid pictures of sleepaway summers more than a half century ago are also blurred with time. Though, like Gail's, my exalted memories of childhood are pristine, present, and ever powerful.

It helps that I still go to Agawak, as the second-to-oldest staff member. Before this comeback, my last stint on staff was in 1973. Margie Gordon, sixty-six and a camp buddy since the old days, works there, too. She takes the youngest girls on overnight camping trips and also teaches yoga. My jobs range from camp historian to alumni coordinator to director of the writing program that produces our Agawak publication, *Agalog*.

The spine of my own photo album is also broken, yet the takeaways from camp form the unbroken spine of my life. Ours is a traditional camp that offers a mix of dozens of land and water sports, and an arts program of handcrafts, dance, music, and theater. In my day, we went for eight straight weeks.

Like most modern full-season camps, Agawak is now divided into two sessions, catering to the rise of youth who need to get home before school begins to train for team sports.

Today, there is a summer camp suited for virtually any child, ranging from those with a focus on film-making, science, circus training, or the performing arts. Most notably in the last category are French Woods, the camp that launched Zooey Deschanel and Adam Levine, and Stagedoor Manor, where Mandy Moore and Natalie Portman got their start.

The smorgasbord of sleepaway camps is varied in rigor and specialty, but camp is camp—a place for children to grow and play. We learn self-care and figure out how to get along with and care for others, away from parental rules and protection. In school we make sequential sets of friends, as we are dispatched to different institutions in the elementary, middle, and upper grades. We see each other in spurts during the day, then go home to our other lives.

While spaced nearly a year apart, weeks spent at camp seem to flow into one continual life, as kids return summer after summer and form relationships that are enduring and substantial. We see each other at our worst and at our best, in tight sleeping quarters, competing in activities, smoothing cabin clashes, reveling in each other's victories, and comforting each other in our defeats.

Immersed in nature and each other, the intimate community of camp offers a whole other kind of education. We learn teamwork, courage, resilience, and empathy, skills of the heart that lay the foundation for transforming camp kids into successful adults, adults who can *deal*.

Nearly all of the twenty-four hundred camps accredited by the American Camp Association ban technology. By disconnecting from texting,

Snapchat, and Instagram, campers learn how to truly connect with each other.

And it turns out, like school, nature can even enhance our brain function. In the book *The Nature Fix: Why Nature Makes Us Happier, Healthier, and More Creative*, the prize-winning author Florence Williams traverses the planet, from the forests of South Korea to the rivers of Idaho, and excavates new research on how nature expands our minds, boosts our moods, and can even reduce the symptoms of ADHD. This is a key discovery in times of mounting childhood depression, anxiety, and attention disorders.

A front-row witness to the restorative perks that come from open sky and open fields, Florence sent her own two children to summer camps.

"Unplugged from technology, studies show that kids who go to camp become better at reading emotions and expressions on people's faces," Florence told me in an interview. "This is a skill that has to be learned and practiced. My children came away from camp feeling very comfortable talking to people of all backgrounds, and of all ages.

"The science shows that the experience of natural beauty makes us feel more connected to each other," she continued. "Nature makes us feel a part of something larger than ourselves. This is a fundamental lesson children need more than ever as they grow up today largely indoors, inundated with social media: that they're not just individuals in a cog; that they need social bonding to grow in all ways. Nature facilitates the shared adventures that form the kernels for deep connections that last a lifetime."

Florence Williams follows the lead of other iconic naturalists who believed the wind and the woods, the mountains and the sea, are a human's best healers. As a summer camp lifer, I know this as deeply as Henry David Thoreau knew it when he wrote *Walden* in the mid-1800s during his two-year two-month two-day retreat to Walden Pond, in the woods near Concord, Massachusetts: "I went to the woods because I wished to live deliberately...I wanted to live deep and suck out all the marrow of life."

When nature surrounds, we dig deeply into self-discovery and our worries can be wiped clean, just like the bare and glisteny bones from which I love to suck clean every trace of marrow, that pungent paste that tastes of the earth.

This is the marrow and this is the life we cannot get anywhere else, no matter how grand are our indoor spaces or how many "friends" we have on Facebook.

Developing these genuine and ongoing relationships is the greatest gift I received of the many gifts from Agawak, a girl gang that became a family, bound not by blood but by history, love, and loyalty.

These friends have tracked me and stuck with me, as a chubby child, a skinny bride, over bumps in raising four sons and staying married to one husband. They have held me up through the sudden death of my father and the long illness of my late mother, and through the recurring sting of an empty nest.

Through rapture and rage, they have met me on the other side, as I have for them, and we are still holding each other up, with sturdy arms and open hearts and with soft shoulders to melt into. We have shared some of the most enchanted hours of our lives, some of the saddest, some of the scariest—all of it.

There is nobody else that knows this about us, that feels all of this for us. Even our mothers and fathers, sisters and brothers, our sons and daughters, partners and spouses, do not know what we know. I speak to a camp friend by phone nearly every day. A lifeline, yes.

These are my people.

These are indestructible relationships cultivated during hundreds of days that started with shivering together in a cold cabin when the morning bell rang and ended with whispering our secrets from our warm beds.

We met as timid youth and grew together from flirty teenagers into a powerful sisterhood that includes some grandmothers. We used to compare bra sizes; we now compare maps of wrinkles.

The transformation that happens in these summers away are immediately noticed by our families. My mom used to say I was so much nicer after two months at camp. Harriet Lowe heard lots of similar stories as the longtime editor in chief of *Camping Magazine*. In her role at the helm of the publication of the American Camp Association, Harriet tapped experts in all areas of camping to pen personal testimonials and share professional expertise on how sleepaway summers impact child development.

Nothing documents that better for Harriet, though, than what she witnesses close up.

"My grandson Corbin, who is seventeen, went to camp from the time he was eight," Harriet tells me. "I truly see how camp changed his life. He is stronger and kinder, more compassionate, confident, and adventurous.

"He says it's his 'happiest place on earth,' and really, that's camp," she adds. "The entire environment is designed totally for kids to have fun, and to climb beyond their comfort zones, to fall and get up again, to become resilient. We have found through our ACA research, that whether the children go for two weeks or the entire summer, they get many of the same benefits across the board: They gain confidence and a real sense of community; they learn to work as a team; they become self-starters; they learn the value of perseverance. My grandson says that he has never been homesick at camp. But when he returns home, he misses camp terribly. We call it 'camp-sick.'"

The social skills learned in real time away from screen time are also the skill set top companies view as markers of a top employee, even by those companies that reign in the computer and tech industry.

Since 2008, Google has conducted a study known as Project Oxygen to explore the hypothesis that what makes for exceptional company managers goes far beyond a superstar background in STEM. Google executives have examined every nugget of personnel data gathered by the company since its 1998 beginnings.

The conclusions of Project Oxygen mirror what you will read in this book about character traits gleaned at summer camp. Among the top markers of a successful career at Google, one of the world's top three brands, are, in corporate lingo, "soft skills," which come from face-to-face interaction: being a good coach; communicating and listening well; creating an inclusive team environment; showing concern for others; being productive and results oriented.

The Partnership for 21st Century Learning, a national coalition of business leaders, educators, and policy makers, underscores Google's findings. Since its inception in 2001, the organization's research points to "the four Cs" as pillars that reinforce professional success: collaboration, communication, critical thinking, and creativity.

These four Cs that lead to achievement in the workplace are lessons also strengthened through the camping experience. I would add two more Cs we get from sleepaway summers—confidence and a desire to contribute to the greater good of a community.

I am not a big organization that has done a far-flung longitudinal study. Yet during several years of long talks with hundreds of camp lovers in researching this book, here is what I know for sure. All these Cs that emerge from official studies come from this overarching C: feeling comfortable in a setting that empowers kids to try new things, to fail, to keep trying, to gain self-esteem from success, to make friends with all sorts of people.

These are skills they start acquiring the minute

they board buses bound for the first summer away from their comfortable nests, to live on their own in rustic lodging, among strangers.

Indeed, becoming independent comes quickly and is key. Camp requires kids to sculpt a life apart from the interference of parents, who can be of the hovering-helicopter or barreling-snowplow varieties.

"Some parents have bubble-wrapped their children, who have the potential to become deeply distracted by technology," says Tom Rosenberg, president and CEO of the American Camp Association. "Camp is an opportunity to unwrap those kids, giving them the chance to engage in human connections and have human-powered adventures, removed from those that are digital-driven.

"Camp is therefore more essential than ever before," Tom continues. "In an era when America's youth are facing a complex landscape of mental, emotional, and social health changes, clearly the social interaction that is a mainstay of camp helps to alleviate the loneliness and depression experienced by more youth today than in the past. While camp life is scheduled, it runs at a slower pace. Kids have time to reflect on who they are, who they want to be, how they may want to change the world. They have time to play and be joyful, and just be kids."

These human-powered adventures continue to seed the social and emotional skills that are essential for victorious grown-up years.

In the ACA's five-year Youth Impact Study completed in 2019, a sample of nearly five hundred former campers, ages eighteen to twenty-five, were asked how their experiences as children at camp played out in school and in their emerging adult lives.

The most consistent outcomes from participants in the study, when asked what was most important in their lives today, which camp played a major role in developing, were: "Relationship skills, independence and responsibility, appreciation for living in the moment, appreciation for diversity, perseverance, and willingness to try new things."

I know from my own experience that these so-called soft skills make for hard workers and stand out for professional recruiters.

Just out of college, with my only prior professional experience being a waitress and a camp counselor, I talked about all of the life skills learned from these challenging jobs during my first interviews. The boss that hired me in an entry-level position at a public relations firm told me later that what I said about getting food orders out fast to impatient diners and herding young girls while being so young myself was a testament to my level of responsibility, people skills, and work ethic.

He said he also appreciated when I shared that I knew the Heimlich maneuver and CPR, in case anyone in the office choked or dropped.

Decades later, I became acquainted with Daniel Goleman's bestseller *Emotional Intelligence*, in which he identifies five major EQ competencies that surmount IQ in forecasting those who will become leaders in the workplace: self-awareness, self-regulation, motivation, empathy, and social skills.

There is no place like camp to build all of the above.

My first year at Agawak, the four other girls in Cabin 3 were a year older. They hung out in two groups of two, and I was the party of one.

Motivated to fit in, I would play jacks alone on

the cabin floor and say that if anyone wanted to join me, I would share my Pez and bubble gum. Bribery eventually got me some respect, as I was really good at jacks and the other girls were impressed I managed to hide the forbidden sweets from our counselors.

This was my toughest camp summer, and the most crucial one in teaching me self-awareness of a resilience I did not know I possessed. This also was an early lesson in developing empathy, another EQ cited by author Goleman, to reach out to other girls who may feel excluded by cliques.

Jill Hirschfield, a camp friend from the 1960s, recalls how learning the art of self-regulation as a young child led to her ability to make smart choices during her university years.

"Camp really helped me adjust easily when I went away to college, because I had already experienced taking care of myself and living with other people," says Jill of her years at the University of Denver. "I was not going crazy with this new-found freedom. Many of my friends from college drank too much and partied too hard, and didn't know how to set their own limits."

While this is a book of lessons and stories that spill from this forever camp girl with forever camp friends, the values and memories are not gender-specific.

I met Bobby Fisher when he was a counselor at our brother camp, Kawaga, and I was a counselor at Agawak—Kawaga spelled backward. Like me, Bobby had spent many years as a camper, and still counts his old bunkmates as among his best friends, a few of whom were groomsmen in his wedding. The sixty-three-year-old entrepreneur who has started many businesses loved Kawaga so much that he and his three brothers bought the camp in 1986.

When Bobby talks about Kawaga, one of the oldest traditional camps in the country, and his achievements from his time as a camper there, his face seems childlike, as if those events happened last week and not forty-five years ago. Three times, Bobby was awarded the highest honor of Wachi Counza, chief of one of the camp's tribes, and was named All-Around Camper.

My emotions swell with understanding as he exudes undying pride from camper victories. Being elected Blue Team captain in 1970 remains one of the crowning achievements of my life. Only a camper gets how these seemingly little things are monumental memories that unfailingly anchor and empower us.

I keep my trophy from winning the Agawak Horse Show on my desk, next to my computer. It reminds me of the black stallion Sailor, who made a perfect jump and rolled into a perfect canter with me on a July afternoon in 1970. With the award in constant viewing range, I feel anew the moment I was given my foot-high silver prize in the shape of a horse, and I laid my head on Sailor's sinewy and sweaty neck.

In my camper days, Agawak and Kawaga and many of the older traditional camps were composed of a population that was nearly all Jewish. The roots of predominantly Jewish summer camps were planted early in the 1900s, led by activist immigrants in the "open air movement" who sought to Americanize their children and provide them with an escape from the heat and filth of industrializing big cities.

By the 1920s, hundreds of these camps had

been established in lush forests and on prime lakeside properties in the United States. While some featured strict religious rituals, most so-called Jewish camps were Jewish only because of their communities and not their practices.

The older traditional camps that historically consisted of mostly Jewish campers are changing. Diversity and inclusion, the two movements that have become the cultural thrust of American educational institutions, are also a central mission of the camping industry. The goal of the American Camp Association is to make it possible for every child who wants to go to camp to have that experience.

Each year, hundreds of children receive financial assistance from the ACA's Send a Child to Camp Fund, and these efforts are slowly turning camps into communities of many different classes and nationalities.

The once-monochromatic Agawak is a committed partner in this mission of "camp for all." The Agawak Alumnae Foundation grants partial and full scholarships every summer, as do many other camps, from those run by the Girl Scouts to the priciest of elite East Coast camps.

While summer camps are undergoing important changes, what I notice most of all in my return to Agawak is that the heart of camp life remains unchanged.

We are one body of girls and women, unified by central wants: We want to have fun. We want to learn from each other. We want to shed our city selves and be sloppy and silly and wild. We want to love and be loved and feel worthy. We want to sing all the time. We want to be together.

A few summers ago, one of my youngest campers, Sadie Benjamin, wrote this poetic testimony to that eternal sentiment, shared from generation to generation:

I walk by girls
Smiling and happy,
And I want to jump, up into the sky, touch the
*   clouds*
And dance around the evening stars,
Throw my head back and laugh aloud with joy
Because I am happy at camp.

My book is about all of this: the songs we don't forget, the friends that make us laugh so hard we cannot breathe, the playfulness we hold on to as we age, and the perseverance we have demonstrated throughout our lives—to try and try again until we get it right.

It is a book about aging well, fortified by lasting love.

May the chapters that unfold be a nostalgic feast for all of us ageless campers, who grow younger with each team song we still sing with our oldest friends, with each marshmallow charred over a fire when making s'mores with our children, and with each memory that throws us back into our finest, most playful of selves.

Even if you never went to camp, though you love to romp in the woods and be free, may this book pull you back to a lake, a cabin, a trail, a mountain, a place of transformative silence and howling laughter and soul-deep relationships.

As I pack for this season at camp that starts in one week, I sort out three piles: one definitely going, one maybe going, one definitely not going. I grab a very old bikini that is thinning at the butt.

I try it on, it looks awful, and I toss it in my duffel. I do not care, and no one else will care, that the taut belly of my camper girlhood is now softened, a leftover from the seventy pounds gained when carrying twin boys, who are now twenty-six.

Camp is camp, a place where what is inside of us is more impressive and inspiring than our exteriors.

Chapter One

Independence

"While summer camp is about communal living, teamwork, and collaboration, the overarching lesson is realizing you need to be a big, strong girl on your own."

Two weeks after the end of third grade, I left the familiar nest of home, bound for the unknown, clutching my teddy bear, Zelda. She was the color of butterscotch and missing an ear. It was late June of 1963, and my sister, Frances, and I boarded an overnight train in Chicago, bound for Camp Agawak, in Minocqua, Wisconsin.

I was eight, and Frances was nine.

At Horace Mann School, in our hometown of Oak Park, Illinois, I had just learned multiplication tables and how to spell big words like "experience." Our parents used the words "fun experience" a lot as we packed our footlockers, huge, clunky things made of plywood tinted teal blue. They fastened with heavy hardware, and were rimmed with brass tacks.

Our mother had hand-sewn labels in every item, and I still have the packing list, which includes a flannel shirt that I still wear. I was a large child.

I loved that my footlocker came with its own key, like my Barbie diary did.

These bulky suitcases, also called "trunks," were used by the military in boot camp and at war, images I had seen on *Combat!*, the gritty TV drama depicting a US platoon during World War II, which our younger brother, Greg, used to watch. Having the same trunk as a soldier gave me a thrill of imminent adventure—and a chill of danger and fright.

When I asked my parents how long we would be gone, a quiver in my voice, my father would distract me by not saying "Eight weeks." Instead, he instructed me to multiply seven times eight.

As June 25 approached, our mom layered precisely folded towels, blankets, sheets, and our blue and white uniform clothing into our footlockers. Witnessing her packing, the upcoming adventure became real, and my fear slackened into antsy anticipation for a fun experience that would last fifty-six days.

That first camp season turned out to be so much fun that it sparked an experience that would last 560 days, over the course of ten summers. And then, decades later, I am back.

At the age of fifty-eight, I returned to work at the camp of my youth, to walk the same woods and swim the same lake in a place where I learned how to be a true and trustworthy friend, and how to trust myself.

I wish I had thanked my mom and dad more for finding Agawak—because the year and a half's worth of days as a camper and counselor would turn out to shape the direction of all of my days, and all of who I am. The nature and freedom and friendships and action that camp offered grabbed me from the start and has never let go.

Though in the last minutes before boarding on that first voyage to my first camp season I was petrified. I clung to my father like a little monkey, holding back tears, as he said over and over: "You're going to love it. It's going to be so much fun. You are a big, strong girl."

I hugged my mother, who was *not* holding back tears. Whenever we left the house, she was afraid she would never see us again. A Polish-born Holocaust survivor, she would have flashbacks of how her immediate family, and seven nieces and nephews, were sent off in trains and never came back.

We were now living in a safe suburb due west of Chicago, in a neighborhood lined with wide sidewalks and maple trees. We were friends with every family on our block. Yet the horror of my mother's past as the orphan of a slaughtered family was a relentless dark shadow.

My first sighting of tattoos was when I was in second grade and I met two of my mom's first cousins, Howard and Jacques, who had survived Auschwitz. Their arms were seared with blue numbers.

Flashbacks of dodging killers never leave a survivor, I learned early on. My sister, brother, and I used to wait for the bus on the curb in front of our house to take us to day camp at the Jewish Community Center. Our mom instructed us to hold our tin lunch boxes in front of our T-shirts, to hide the brown JCC lettering. She was afraid an anti-Semitic stranger would stop by in a car and whisk us away.

When we were growing up, the population in Oak Park was largely Catholic and Protestant, with only about 2 percent Jewish families. Our family was not Orthodox in religious practices, but given our mother's history, our parents were vehement that we identify with a Jewish community. So they started that immersion early, enrolling their three children in a JCC camp at kindergarten age.

One of my first lucid memories is eating a peanut-butter-and-grape-jelly sandwich at that camp, seated at a picnic table in the woods. The peeling paint was rubbing my thighs, exposed by shorts. Swatting mosquitoes, I was hot but content. I ate quickly, so I could resume running through sprinklers and playing Red Rover in the large field.

When I think of the word "camp" now, a word that conjures up play and freedom, I am reminded that not that long ago that word meant slave labor, incarceration, and evil.

My mother died thirteen years ago, and it is only now that I think of asking her how she felt about the word "camp." For her children, the word meant recreation. When she was in Poland, the age of an American girl headed for a sleep-away summer, the word meant death.

In dispatching us to Agawak, our parents followed the wave of Jewish immigrants before and after World War II who sent their children out of crowded cities to live communally in nature. And many of those Jewish parents went on to be the founders of dozens more of the oldest sleep-away camps in the United States still in operation seventy-five years or longer.

Agawak was started by Chicagoan Flora Pinkhurst in 1921. In a 1946 *Chicago Tribune* article on the wave of city kids fleeing the sweltering summers to the woods of Wisconsin, Agawak was cited for having lake water so pure it was "used for drinking."

Blue Lake is still very clean, and the perch, bass, and walleye are abundant, but I drink from the faucets, like we did as kids. The campers now drink from pastel metallic water bottles, attached to them like appendages.

Decades before the flight of Jewish immigrants into the American woods, it was actually the Christian men who launched the summer-camp trend. In 1885, the Young Men's Christian Association opened Camp Dudley for boys on Lake Champlain in New York, still standing as the oldest continuously running summer camp in the country. By 1916, the number of boys attending YMCA camps had climbed to close to twenty-four thousand. Wisconsin is home to more than one hundred of those camps, such as Phantom Lake YMCA Camp, founded in 1896, and one of America's earliest camps.

Summer camps for girls were established early in the twentieth century. The nondenominational

Camp Kehonka, in Wolfeboro, New Hampshire, came first, with its opening in 1902. It closed after a run of eighty-three years. During the next several years, the Girl Scouts and Camp Fire Girls started up dozens of camps along the lakes of the Northeast and Midwest, of which many are still in existence.

Jennifer Manguera was a Girl Scout from kindergarten through tenth grade. During her elementary school years, she spent two weeks each summer at Camp Butterfly, in southern Missouri. At the age of fifty, she is now a Girl Scout leader and works at Camp Brighton Woods in Maryland. When she talks about her childhood as a Girl Scout camper, her memories mirror the American Camp Association studies that conclude that the sleepaway experience makes a multifaceted imprint, whether sessions run two or eight weeks.

JENNIFER

Whether you are living in the woods for one day or several weeks, you gain important life skills. You are learning how to cope on your own, away from home for the first time. You are learning how to get along with a group of kids you just met. If someone is mean to you, you can't say "Mom, take care of this." You have to do your own talking.

You are learning the importance of serving others when you are part of connecting with a community 24/7. This is a connection you don't even get at home with your family, unless you are snowbound. The lessons learned and friendships formed through living in the woods in a tent with strangers for a few weeks of my life have been fundamental lessons in becoming independent, in problem-solving, in relationships, and in all aspects of life. Because of camp, I will always be respectful of the earth. Songs that inspired me in my youth I still teach girls, like "Can a Woman Fly an Airplane? Yes, She Can!" We learned to really live the Girl Scouts' pledge: "To help people at all times."

Many friends my age who did not go to camp often tell me they thought it was only the rich Jewish girls who had that luxury. I love informing them that it was Cooper Ballentine, an ex–church choirboy, who built Camp Kehonka, and that it was the Girl Scouts and Camp Fire Girls, of diverse economic and cultural classes, that pioneered the trend of sleepaway summers for girls.

The oldest Jewish camps in the nation, as well, were hardly a haven for the very rich. Like Surprise Lake Camp in Cold Spring, New York, they were for the kids of factory-working immigrants. Surprise Lake was created in 1902 to give Jewish boys from the tenements of New York City's Lower East Side a free summer away from the sweatshops where they would otherwise be working with their parents. Its first year in operation, Surprise Lake Camp had six tents, five counselors, and twenty-five campers.

Surprise Lake grew into a nonprofit institution with a current population of five hundred boys and girls, and it continues to offer scholarships for half of its campers.

Some of those benefiting from Surprise Lake's philanthropy throughout its 110-year history include celebrities such as Eddie Cantor, Jerry Stiller, and Larry King, and my friend Heidi Marcus Katz, who met her husband, Bruce, on the waterfront when they were both on staff as teens.

"We had this special spot where we sat together

at night. It was pitch black, and we would look up at the stars," Heidi recalls. "I knew who he was before our romance began. He was the skinny kid with glasses, and I had no interest. I skipped a couple of summers, and when I came back, I saw this handsome lifeguard and said to my friends, 'Who is that big hulk over there?'

"Bruce had filled out. He was six feet tall. He had long hair. I followed him to college in Maryland and never left his side since."

Heidi, sixty-three and raised in Queens, began as a scholarship camper at Surprise Lake starting in the late 1960s, followed by her two younger brothers, also granted tuition funds. Her father was a postman and her mother worked as a freelance bookkeeper.

"You have no idea what camp meant to a working-class family," Katz tells me. "I grew up in a one-bedroom apartment that housed five of us. Only the bedroom had air-conditioning. We all ate and slept in that bedroom all summer. And there were lots of campers with worse circumstances than us. From that, we went to the extravagance of sleeping in cabins in the cool mountain air. Oh my God, it was exhilarating. We were transported out of the hot, dirty city into a different world."

Like at Surprise Lake, when my sister and I began our Agawak summers in the sixties, all the girls were Jewish except two. Unlike at Surprise Lake, the majority of campers were from the affluent northern suburbs of Chicago. Our hometown of Oak Park was mostly middleclass, and lots of our friends' parents worked night shifts in factories and hospitals. Moms were sturdy, not fancy.

As Frances and I waited to board the train, I noticed that many of the mothers had primped more than ours; I fixated on one with a platinum-blond Twiggy cut, tight white pants, and white sandals with spiky high heels. The white poodle she was holding had a collar of pink rhinestones.

Our mother was wearing navy culottes and a red-checked blouse ordered from the Sears catalog, and just a bit of lipstick. We had a guinea pig as a pet, not a dog. I can still picture my mom near the tracks: understated, natural, and, I thought, beautiful. I also remember that my sister and I, though from an upper-middle-class upbringing, felt different right away.

Our father grew up poor during the Depression, the son of the first Russian-born doctor to settle in Chicago. My grandfather's patients were mostly struggling immigrants, so he would regularly get salamis or strudels as payment instead of money.

My dad put himself through Northwestern University and started a cabinet company in the late 1940s. His business grew over the decades into a large manufacturer of furniture that encased computers, coffee makers, and copy machines.

Still, both of our parents retained a Depression-era mentality, always Sears over Saks, Oldsmobiles over Cadillacs. Our first year at Agawak, tuition was $750 for the eight weeks. Today, a full eight-week season at Agawak costs closer to $10,000. This is the lower side of tuitions compared to some of the exclusive East Coast full-season camps, where parents can shell out upwards of $12,000 for a whole summer.

Frances and I knew that the $1,500 it cost to send us both to camp was a lot of money, and it corroborated our sense that we were about to enter an exotic new land. As we waved out the window and the train pulled away, we could not see our parents in a view darkened by dusk. We were dressed in the camp uniform—navy-blue slacks, powder-blue collared shirts, and navy cardigan sweaters.

My sister recently reminded me that when we slept on the train, me on the top bunk, her on bottom, I dangled my arm down so we could be touching each other's fingers until we fell asleep.

What I could never imagine more than a half century later was that I would birth four sons who would also spend many summers at sleepaway camp. And I would feel just like my mother felt—afraid to let them go. So during the several summers they spent at Raquette Lake Boys Camp in the Adirondacks of upstate New York, I went with them, to work on staff.

This choice was as much about staying close to my children as it was about the opportunity to get back into the woods, to get back into a cold lake, to laugh and sing in a dining hall. I also got the benefit of tuition remission as compensation at this high-end camp, instead of taking a salary.

I served as the group leader for the youngest boys and created the camp newspaper, the *Daily*

Raquette. My husband, Chuck, built a carpentry shop and launched the woodworking program.

The campers called him Wood Chuck. I still do.

Over many summers spent living on Raquette Lake, I became close friends with staff members at our sister camp across the lake. Many of them were Raquette Lake alumni, and during our nights out at the local bar, they would tell stories from the cabins they grew up in together, about the thrills of the competition during Color Wars, and reminisce about the counselors they worshipped during their shared girlhood.

One night, we were sitting at an outdoor table, and they were talking about how, as campers, they would heave with sobs the last night of camp, and how sad they were now on this night, even as counselors, as camp was almost over. They started to sing one of their old camp songs, "Pine Trees":

Like a glowing ember
Our memories linger on
Mid sighs and tears
Yet we will choose to never lose
The friendships we've made here

It was a breezy night with a flawless sky splashed with stars. The setting and the nostalgia stirred up from a song of lasting friendship threw me back to the hundreds of nights I sat with my forever friends at Agawak, singing around a campfire, under the stars.

A stranger to their Raquette Lake memories, I left the table and started to cry, fixated on *my* camp roots, planted not in the mountains of the Adirondacks but in the flatlands of Wisconsin. That was my home. Eventually, I found my way back.

This return happened at Agawak's ninetieth reunion, when the camp's owner, Mary Fried, told me she had read one of my books. I credited *Agalog* as the launchpad of my literary career, and she responded with a puzzled look, "What's *Agalog*?"

With the vein in my neck throbbing, spit flying, I went on and on about the camp publication that had died decades earlier. I explained that I had worked at Raquette Lake running a newspaper that I had founded to replicate *Agalog*.

Nearly in the same breath, Mary said, "Would you ever want to come back and…" as I said, "What if I came back and…" We know instantly those people who are meant to be in our lives. Mary is one of them—a soul sister who also has camp at her core.

We hugged each other hard, and *Agalog* was reborn. And with its resurrection I, too, have been reborn.

My children are raised, my husband is flexible and loyal. The sense of independence and creativity that camp continues to build in me is the nucleus of my well-being—as it has always been.

As a child, I would steal away to a secluded bench on the waterfront to compose articles and poems on camp stationery, treasuring the silence and solitude. I loved the aloneness, writing what I wanted without the crowding of classmates' desks and without a teacher doling out assignments and grades.

I wrote this poem at the age of nine, in the summer of 1964:

We're here at Agawak, a camp so dear
We can run and be free because we are here
Agawak is a camp where it is fun
We work and play in the rain or sun

We all love it so very much
And there isn't another camp as such.

A rough start, but, hey, it rhymes. At the end of a camp week, which included five periods a day of land and water sports, we downshifted into the Sunday night ritual of the reading of *Agalog*. Oscar, the camp director, would sit in front of the fireplace in our central log lodge and read aloud all of the entries.

Agalog was pieced together on large construction paper, with covers depicting primitive nature scenes and portraits made by campers in Arts & Crafts. I remember that those pots of thick paints in primary colors smelled really good, and I loved how they swirled onto paper off the bristles of my brush.

Stories were written on a manual typewriter, then cut out and taped onto the pages. Each week, the publication was devoted to one of various themes that reflected character traits campers would develop during the summer, including leadership, loyalty, kindness, courage, and sportsmanship.

Paging through old issues of *Agalog*, I see that the traits born of the camp experience and fleshed out in those old articles have scripted this long life—and inspired this book.

Then, the camp was composed of 120 girls, less than half the population of its community today. On *Agalog* nights, we would sprawl on the dusty wooden floor of the lodge in our puffy chenille bathrobes, quietly braiding each other's hair. It was the only time there was no raucous yelling or laughing. We were rapt as Oscar shared the simple words of contributors. The only other sound was the fire crackling.

I wrote every week, and what a high I was on, heartened by a rush of recognition, each time Oscar would say, "And this article is by Iris Krasnow." Older campers and counselors would offer praise as we shuffled back to our cabins, in furry slippers caked with dirt.

Decades later, as some of my books have climbed onto bestseller lists, I credit those first fans for their encouraging reviews. That initial praise from people I admired coupled with a passion for my craft turned out to be a potent and lasting combination.

I credit my sister, Frances, most of all, for setting me on my lifelong career path: She was always the first to run up to me and say "You are really good at this." I believed her and kept at it.

Bringing back *Agalog*, I am witness to the same emancipation I felt as a budding author. I see campers with yellow pads in their laps, nestled in a pine forest, heads down, their pens racing across the page. Away from the confines of a classroom and a teacher's steely gaze, open air opens every sense, every pore.

I give lots of guidance and effusive compliments, which builds self-assurance far more than grades.

In times of my own self-doubt, blocked and staring at a blank computer screen, I close my eyes and imagine myself as a child, on that bench near Blue Lake, writing freely from a primal place. Now, I am the adult in the woods telling young girls doubting the quality of their works, "You are really good at this." And it is me sitting in a chair at the Sunday night campfire, reading the campers' essays and poems and watching the proud smiles as the writers hear their names.

The self-esteem I gained from writing made those first summers at camp far less lonely. My thoughts were a comforting companion, amplified in depth and clarity in nature, where I was able to access and express the subtlest timbres in my voice.

My campers today tell me the same thing, that writing in nature elicits an unleashing of spirit unmatched in a school setting. An Agawak camper for the past five summers, Madeline Glazier, wrote this ode to her love of words at the age of eleven:

The flick of a page.
Words in the air.
Images in my head
Come alive
Agalog is something to look
Forward to every fourth period
A tunnel into happiness
A portal on paper.
Peace is found within
A spiritual event.

"Writing under a big sky, I am so much more tuned in to what is going on in my head and heart," says Madeline. "Nothing is restraining me."

When my sister and I talk about being sent to camp when we were Madeline's age on an overnight train without our parents, we are incredulous that we did it—that they did it—without mobile phones.

In the first hour of the rollicky ride, we talked loudly to each other to drown out the crying of a red-faced girl nearby and her shouts of: "I want to go hoooommme!"

Any homesickness we felt was assuaged by a new friend, Gina, sitting across from us. My curly hair was freshly shorn, and I envied her long ponytail, sleek and straight.

I also envied the small brown paper bag in her lap, from which she had just pulled out a couple of Bulls-Eyes, soft caramels with vanilla-cream centers. At my age, I do not always remember what I ate for dinner the previous night, but I remember in delicious detail how Gina slowly unwrapped a caramel, put it in her mouth, and chewed slowly, with an expression that seemed otherworldly.

She must have noticed my coveting stares, because she offered to share some of the candy her mom had packed: multicolored dots on paper strips and little wax bottles filled with sugary liquid.

Chewing off the tiny sweet dots, my sister and I realized that camp might really be what Daddy had said it would be: "a lot of fun." While counselors would be supervising us, they were not our parents, and we could diverge from home rules. For one, it looked like we could eat candy before dinner, something that was forbidden at home.

The strings of red licorice that came next further lessened any lingering thoughts of the increasing distance between us and our parents.

Learning at a young age to cope independently with a brave face, even if it is feigned at first, is a key formative lesson I took from camp, just as Girl Scout leader Jennifer Manguera did. At the end of the first summer, I had pushed through many fears, among them, night frights.

During many times in early childhood, eerie thoughts would shake me awake, like green monsters with fangs about to take a chunk out of my leg, and bearded men holding sacks over their shoulders to hurl me into. I would plod across the hall to my parents' room and shake my father awake. He would bring me a glass of warm milk laced with honey, then lull me to sleep with a song from the one-week YMCA camp he attended on scholarship for two summers in the late 1920s, which began like this: *"Camp Duncan, you know, is the best place to go, in the good old summertime. The grass is so green, the water so clean, oh, how we love it so."*

He would tell us that those two weeks at camp held some of his happiest boyhood memories. Located in Ingleside, Illinois, an hour and change from downtown Chicago, Camp Duncan is still going strong as it nears its hundredth birthday.

In a cabin on a dark hill at Agawak, far away from my dad's singing and room service, when night frights hit, I had to soothe myself. "We're all right. Don't be scared," I would whisper to my teddy bear. And when cabinmates excluded me, I learned how to turn within for solace and for strength.

At camp, I found that if you acted brave, you felt brave, a lesson I have carried with me ever since.

Camp did turn me into a big, strong girl, then a big, strong woman who knows how to get things done on her own. I learned to be alone without feeling lonely.

In one of my first letters home, I wrote:

Dear Mommy and Daddy, The nights are cold. The counselors are old. They are not as old as you, but don't worry! I am taking care of myself.

I learned to take care of myself at camp in the 1960s, and I am still learning to do this now, as I have lost both parents and my grown sons have left the nest. While summer camp is about communal living, teamwork, and collaboration, the overarching lesson is realizing you need to be a big, strong girl on your own.

Always.

Most in my circle of adult camp girls have lost one or both parents; many have lost siblings and friends. We are greatly fortified by our Agawak conditioning to carry on through adversity, sure-footed, self-reliant, hopeful.

After my father died suddenly at sixty-seven in 1986, killed by the wrong drug administered to treat a heart attack, I signed up to help lead a group of children with muscular dystrophy, spina bifida, and cerebral palsy on a mountain-climbing expedition in Yosemite National Park. We roped up with the kids and rappelled with them down the peaks.

I had never rappelled or climbed a tall mountain before. It was the spirit of camp that lifted me out of unthinkable agony and pushed me forward, giving me a willingness to carry on, to take risks, to stand on my own. It was confidence stemming from camping trips and my counselor experience that drew me to an opportunity to lead and help children who needed a lot of help, in the glory of nature.

When I was eleven, Agawak counselor Debbie used to comfort us during bouts of missing our parents with: "Remember who you are." When we remember who we were as campers, we can channel that camp-girl spirit to remember who we are today: capable of forging onward, through anything.

Living away from my parents and learning to stand on my own as a child has made all the losses and disappointments in life more bearable. This priceless gift from camp has become a wellspring for survival. Because, inevitably, as we accumulate birthdays, loved ones die, children leave home, and we must know how to stand alone.

When I was seventeen, I was safe amid the birch and pine trees of Agawak, as the counselor of a cabin filled with adoring ten-year-olds.

When my mother was seventeen, she was orphaned and in hiding.

She used to say that no matter how many loving people we have in our lives, those people could be snatched from us in a finger snap. And that the most important love to nurture, the only one that lasts, is a love of self.

She was not a narcissist. She was a realist.

My mother learned in her youth what we all come to know as we age: that we can have the best families and the best of friends, yet the most important person to learn to count on is ourselves. I learned this at home, and this was solidified at camp: Independence and self-sufficiency are the most critical of traits.

Chapter Two

Community

"This is perhaps the most fundamental lesson from camp: an ability to adapt to communal living and form friendships with people far different than me."

I am seated at the Baltimore Amtrak station, bound for New York City, and the woman next to me, about my age, points to her large flowered canvas bag and asks, "Will you watch this for me? I'm going to the bathroom. I'll be quick."

Normally, I would not watch a stranger's belongings, particularly in this climate, when we hear booming voices on speakers at airports and train stations about the dangers of "unattended baggage." Yet this woman was so smiley and seemingly so normal, and I said, "Sure."

She was back in less than two minutes, and, laughing, I observed: "You must have gone to summer camp. Camp girls learn how to pee fast in the woods."

"Yes! Loved, loved camp!" she responded loudly, her eyes lighting up.

I may never see this woman again, who was a camper in the Berkshires for ten summers as a child. Yet as we reminisced about putting frogs in our counselors' beds and Color Wars and using leaves as toilet paper on canoe trips, I felt more connected to her than I do with some friends I have known for years.

"My camp friends are still my best friends," we said almost in unison as we boarded and went our separate ways.

I'm strong for Camp Agawak, the place where the breezes sway. No matter the weather, we will all stick together. This stanza from one of Agawak's signature songs has proven to be true. Camp girls who grow up together during sleepaway summers stick together throughout all the seasons of our lives.

Pushing our bodies in the water and on fields and on courts through fierce matches of tennis and volleyball, we repeatedly ascend to new athletic heights. Yet the most important victory, season after season, is how camp enlarges our capacity for loyalty and love, continuing long after our camper years end.

Camp also enlarges our capacity to handle strife. When a cabin fight erupts, we learn how to talk it out and move on, not simmer. We learn how to forgive. We learn the value of a sincere apology.

I continue to be a student of those lessons that are amplified in a camp setting.

More than a half century has passed since I was new to Agawak, and I am still walking those woods and swimming Blue Lake with my wild and devoted camp-girl tribe, who visit camp often. And I am witness to the next generation of camp girls forming their own tribal unity, persevering when their friendships are tested, as some of ours were over time.

As I watch young campers replicating our historic ritual at the Sunday campfire—standing and swaying and singing "Friends, friends, friends—we will always be, the truest, the finest..."—my entire life hurls through me.

I am eight, and I am sixty-four.

Through a lens illuminated by waves of gratitude and nostalgia, I see what these young girls have yet to realize—that new friends will turn into old friends who will become the thread that stitches all the pieces of their lives together.

Like a perfect quilt.

In this rendition at Agawak, awash with memories yet fully awake in the now, I am constantly, soothingly reminded that the line between past and present is a flimsy filament that can be broken at any moment to fuse into one unbroken life.

This life that feels whole is substantial and new, and is something I have yearned for throughout the scattered passages already lived.

Often as an *Agalog* activity, I have the girls write letters home. On Visiting Weekend, parents extol how meaningful it is to receive handwritten notes from their children. They are used to seeing impersonal printouts from computers, which are banned for Agawak campers. I hear from these mothers and fathers that their girls express as much, or more, excitement about their deepening friendships as they do about getting up on water skis for the first time.

I, too, often wrote about friendship in letters home and in my articles for *Agalog*, as in this dispatch from 1965, when I was the junior editor:

> *Something that causes inspiration can be beautiful, fun or spiritual. My friends at Agawak bring me all of these things. We will be together through happiness and heartbreak for a very long time.*

Prophetic words from a ten-year-old.

Whereas school and hometown friends may drift away, I have never lost a close camp friend, including those from my few summers on Raquette Lake. Camp is the breeding ground for relationships that are cemented by physical closeness, emotional maturation, psychic fulfillment—and hilarious fun.

Gayle Ulmann, sixty-one, is an integral part of my friend group from my summers on staff at Raquette Lake Boys Camp. She is the leader of the oldest group of campers across the lake, at Raquette Lake Girls Camp, a position she has held for the past twenty-one years. Gayle is also a third-grade teacher in Great Neck, New York, the town where she was raised, and where she raised three sons.

Like me, Gayle, the only woman in an all-male house, relishes her escapes into the summer sisterhood. She elaborates on the unique quality of camp friendship and the fun factor found nowhere else.

GAYLE

I have strong female friendships at home stemming from a young age, but still it is different at camp. What we develop at camp has a quality that is so freeing and so rare. At camp, I can be totally myself. I can put on stupid costumes. I can be very silly and childish. I hug everyone. Can you imagine hugging people on the streets of New York City? You'd be arrested.

When I laugh with camp friends, it is a laughter that is long and deep and real. Our friendships just seem so natural, nothing is forced, we are intricately connected, heart to heart, solidified by a very close community.

I have three sons and grew up with three brothers. Coming from two houses of all men, camp has taught me so much about what it means to be a woman. I have discovered this female sensitivity in myself I didn't know existed and that I feel everywhere at camp. I find myself crying when candles are lit during camp ceremonies or when girls are singing a certain camp song.

When I'm with my friends at Raquette Lake, I don't even have to say what's on my mind or how I am feeling—my camp sisters know it. No one understands a camp girl like another camp girl.

When I tell my friends at home I'm going back to camp, they say, "What are you, crazy?" If they only knew how wonderful this kind of crazy fun, crazy love feels.

Every camp girl turned camp woman I have known or interviewed echoes Gayle's sentiment: It is great to be around all girls, easier to feel free, to "let it all hang out," a reference to the 1967 Hombres song that we used to dance to at camp socials and that no young camper today likely has ever heard.

The power of our impact on each other's growth and sense of self-worth is corroborated by numerous sociological and psychological studies that have tracked the benefits of same-sex education. And while methods and the scope of surveys may vary, this one conclusion is common: Girls generally blossom more comfortably and more fully in environments void of the inhibiting factor of the opposite sex.

With decreased self-consciousness that may impact learning and performance, girls are also free to express their tight bonds and affection without fear of being judged.

What Gayle said about the bounty of hugs she gives and gets are interactions I, too, love about camp, and what I miss most when I leave. The human touch in real time is irreplaceable as a show of love. Though we do count on FaceTime to keep our far-flung circle of camp girls closely connected when we are not together.

I have been friends with Terry Rubin since 1966, when we met on the bus ride from Chicago to Minocqua. We spent several summers together in Blue Lake, on the Blue Team, and living in the same bunks. Terry stayed in Denver after attending college there. A nurse and office manager in her husband's pediatric practice, Terry has not been able to attend all of our reunions. We have seen each other only a dozen or so times since we left each other at the bus stop in 1970, our final year as campers. During the December holidays, she sent me this text: "Iris, we are in the third trimester of our lives—we need to spend time together now."

That line served as an urgent slap to start an hour-and-a-half FaceTime chat. She is sixty-four, like me, and we were instantly eleven again.

Our love felt as real and voluminous as when we slept inches away from each other all those summers, all those decades ago, when we always made sure our beds were next to each other. Now, she skimmed the phone over her tattoos, one a pink ribbon marking that she has beaten breast cancer, another a vine of aspen leaves crawling up her right shoulder.

She showed me photos of her three children, now all doctors like her husband, and her four grandchildren.

We are old and we are young and we are so much more in between, layers of time and mischief and dancing on the edges. She reminds me that in Cabin 12, we were part of a devilish girl gang that locked a cabinmate in the closet. We said profuse "I'm sorrys" to her at a camp reunion decades later.

We always pulled each other back to solid ground, and we still do as we endure tough passages, 1,700 miles apart. We chose good spouses. We raised good families. I tell Terry, one of the fastest runners in Agawak history, that to me she will always be Olympic Queen, a title she earned our last year as campers, for winning the most races on Olympic Day.

I cry when we hang up, and book a ticket to fly to Colorado the following month, for a hug in real time.

Those hugs meant everything as children, and they still do in my silver-haired years.

On any given day at camp, I can get upwards

of seventy hugs, some from eight-year-olds who barely make it to my waist, others from teens who top my five feet eight. And there are lots of embraces from fellow staff members.

We hug each other good morning at flag raising, and we hug each other in passing to our activities that cover our more than two hundred acres. We hug each other when we meet again at the flagpole before dinner, and we hug each other good night.

I love the feeling of a long hug, one that crushes my body with a force that means something. A hard hug conveys "You are valuable to me." A hug at camp can heal even a wicked quarrel.

When I first met Liz Klein Glass fifteen years ago on the playground where our children attended school, the chemistry was instant, as we realized we were both camp girls forever. That initial encounter between two strangers ended in a lengthy hug.

Liz, now fifty, grew up in Baltimore and spent many summers with her twin sister at Camp Wohelo in Waynesboro, Pennsylvania, which closed in 1987. Their mother had attended Wohelo as well, for a decade, beginning in the mid-1940s.

Liz and I often say that no matter what shifts in our worlds, camp friendships endure.

Liz recalls that she and her twin sister felt like Wohelo girls years before they arrived, due to a mom who sang camp songs throughout their childhood and talked incessantly about camp traditions. Wearing her old uniform T-shirt, printed with Camp Wohelo and a picture of a Native American princess, Liz builds upon the irrepressible spirit of all-girl power:

LIZ

My mother, who is eighty-four, still sings Wohelo songs. With her increasing dementia, she doesn't always remember my name. But she knows she was captain of the White Team and All-Around Camper in 1951. And she is still in touch with her camp friends—those that are still alive!

Without a doubt, camp friends are best friends. There is no one else who has the depth of this shared history. We have huge memories, like winning Color Wars, and lit-

tle ones, like eating cookies and milk together every night at the flagpole, and shredding our camp T-shirts so we could look like we came off the set of Flashdance.

We used to sit on the porch of our cabin and shave our legs as a group. You would never do that if boys were around.

There's something about being with all girls all the time. There is none of the social pressure to look pretty or to suppress your personalities. We were just girls, walking around or skipping, holding hands and singing. We wore uniforms, so though our bodies were obviously different, everyone kind of looked the same.

Here we were hugging all the time, and not having it mean anything other than love. There was no talk of "Oh, you're so gay," which kids would have said back in school in the early 1980s. In first grade, I may have held hands with classmates, but not after ninth grade, like we did at camp.

At school, I was a student. At home, I was a daughter. At camp, there are no roles you have to play. Your job at camp is to grow and have fun and be open to people different than you but who are all there for the same purpose.

Your whole soul opens up at camp.

We had a reunion on the Jersey Shore with my camp friends who are now in their forties and fifties. Some of us have not seen or spoken to each other for years. In the first five minutes, it felt like we had never left camp. That is real friendship.

In my own reunions with camp friends, a disparate group of women—skinny, chunky, bookish, sporty, shy, and untamed—we also feel instantly unified. We are locked in a shared and unfurling timeline, etched with lots of challenges.

We dressed alike, in blue and white, and slept in cold cabins with no hot water and one smelly "geek," as we called the single-stall bathroom. We grew into an unbreakable family.

Camp often felt like an idyllic utopia, but like any community that consists of close human relationships, there are conflicts and imperfections. Camp girls form tight circles of love and trust, but they can also be really mean. There are cliques formed in cabins; some girls reign and others are left out. While we suffered through brief breakups, we always came back together.

From the hard times, the sad times, the lonely

times, and the uncomfortable times came transformative moments that released a newfound ability and urgency to spring back, to learn negotiating skills, to figure out how to fit in, to develop grit—all without parents.

The ability to excavate our inner strength in times of adversity is something camp girls often reflect upon at our reunions, as we are tossed back into tough face-offs at camp: remembering friends-turned-enemies or failing at a sport. This is the gift that keeps on giving as we mature and face bigger challenges with our families, our work, our social circles, and all the stressors that mount as we age.

Throughout it all, we grow.

Emboldened by our sisterhood, we form selves that are more real and expansive than those prescribed, and often limited, at home and in school.

"Anything seemed possible at sleepaway camp," says Terry Worth, a close camp friend. She spent twelve summers at Agawak beginning at age nine, seven as a camper and five as a staff member, culminating with the position of assistant water-front director.

"I was this little nebbish when I started camp, a gawky, nonathletic kid," she tells me. "At camp, I flourished. I was popular. I felt like I had everyone cheering for me, and I was everyone's cheerleader."

I was Terry's counselor when she was in the oldest group of girls, who lived in Cabin 15. Over the years, I had witnessed her metamorphosis into a brave teen and a multitalented sportswoman, particularly excelling in the water and as a sharpshooter. Terry remains one of only two girls in Agawak's near hundred years to earn an expert badge in riflery. That meant she was an expert shot while sitting, kneeling, and standing.

Though Terry did rise to become one of Agawak's most beloved campers and counselors and top achievers, memories of her rocky start linger on. She recalls that first summer in the youngest cabin with girls who dwarfed her in height—and self-esteem—and how she steered her journey upward.

TERRY

Talk about challenges, not only was I the shortest in the cabin, I was placed with three girls who were all so confident, and I was this geeky kid. One girl was one of the most beautiful I had ever seen. Another's dad was part owner of the camp. And another was the leader of the cabin, and grew up to become captain of the White Team.

I was insecure and sad for the first couple of weeks. So at the age of nine, I started on this journey, which has really become a lifelong journey, to be proud of who I am and not compare myself to other people.

I was always the funny one, and still am—the person who lifts people up, the person who can always make others laugh. The funny one: This is my trademark. I'm the backup music, the Rhoda to the Mary Tyler Moores. I give the impression that things roll off my back, though some things from camp hit me harder than my friends realized.

As a joke, my nickname became Terry Worthless, a play on my last name of Worth. I embraced this nickname as a sign that I was being noticed. I laughed about it, though deep down it had an effect on my insecurity.

That nickname remained through all of my camper and counselor years.

There are traces of that insecure little girl still in this sixty-year-old woman. But Terry Worthless, the Rhoda, ended up just fine.

Over the years, I worked hard and became very successful at camp. I became the assistant waterfront director, coaching others in their pursuits toward swimming and diving goals. I turned into a brave nature girl and helped lead difficult canoe trips to Canada.

I was never much of a self-promoter. I call myself a quiet winner, who did end up shining. After all of this, I do believe I am Terry Worthy, and my biggest strength remains that I'm a person who can always make others feel stronger.

I wasn't always the leader. I wasn't a team captain. But I always felt respected and appreciated. I always felt loved. As I got much older, I realized that while I was loved by my parents, it was conditional love at home. Even though we had all these rules at camp, the love was unconditional. It was absolutely our own little village. I came away from those summers realizing so much more about who I am and who I can be. Most of all, I came away from camp knowing how to be a true friend.

When we pull up to camp for our reunions, we all have the same expression on our faces that speaks of relief, an expression that says "I am home." I'm five feet tall, but at camp I felt like a giant.

Terry is part of my core group of Agawak alumni that spend a long weekend at camp while I am there. She routinely brings up how our shaky starts decades ago turned into a solid sense of well-being because of our support for one another. We talk about reeling from our first time away from parents, first bras, first crushes after socials with boys from Kawaga. We replay how great it felt to make up after stupid cabin feuds.

The emotional support that women give each other is also obvious in so many other longstanding friend circles I have observed beyond that of grown camp girls. From relationships that evolved in all-women's colleges or in homes with lots of sisters to what I saw in my own mother, the enrichment we give each other is life-changing.

I remember my mother's sharply shifting moods as a housewife with three young children in the middle 1960s. Often when I returned home from school, she would be doing crossword puzzles and smoking Kents and sighing so deeply her shoulders would heave. Other afternoons she would be giggly, hugging me harder than usual, singing French love songs while making meatloaf, whipping the red-striped kitchen towel through the air like a Flamenco dancer.

On Helene Krasnow's happiest days, it inevitably turned out she had played Scrabble with her friend Shirley down the street, or had clustered with other neighborhood moms to plan a PTA fund-raiser. "The girls," as she called them, never failed to lift her, and although we never talked about it, I realized early on that her circle of "girls" was an escape from the relentless tugs of three kids; they affirmed her self-esteem and identity in ways my father, who worked from 8:30 a.m. to 5:30 p.m. at an office a forty-five-minute drive away, could not.

A woman knows best what it is like to live in another woman's skin. There is something about summer that intensifies those bonds. With lots of sun and warmth and room to move, we are like plants that spread and climb in all directions. Along with the great weather spurring our flowering, we coaxed each other through the tunnels of youth, going in as timid girls in the dark, and coming out as feisty and enlightened women.

Many of us got our first periods during those summers of change, and were coached by older girls from outside the bathroom stalls on how to graduate from bulky Modess pads to tiny tampons, way better for swimming.

Our bonds continued to thicken through celebrating the birth of children, graduations, the birth of grandchildren—and a switch from Modess to Depends. Our bonds were also deepened by sorrow, as we have grieved together through surgeries and the deaths of siblings and parents and marriages.

We were there for Terry Worth, through a painful divorce, three hip replacements, and a great remarriage. We were there for Jill Hirschfield, when several years ago, with no family history, she was diagnosed with stage-two breast cancer. As she tells it, the loving shield of sisterhood support greatly eased the journey.

JILL

My first phone calls were to two camp sisters who also had battled breast cancer. Shortly after, I got an envelope in the mail. In it was a pair of Wonder Woman bikini underwear, a reminder of my strength. Every time I opened my underwear drawer in the morning, it made me smile. It made me know: I can do this.

Throughout this hard journey, my camp friends rallied around me. They sent food. They bought me a beautiful nightgown and robe. They were just present, always, in a reassuring way. These friendships have always given me an inner strength to believe: I can do this. We learn at camp to be adaptable and also to be tough. That has helped enormously in adulthood, to not feel like a victim but to feel you can push through almost anything—with a lot of help from our friends.

No matter the weather, we did all stick together, through the fluctuating temperatures of our psyches, through "happiness and heartbreak," as my childhood *Agalog* article predicted.

Camp is the refuge where we fled to be healed and upheld by our friends. We are a reliable resource for each other to transport us back into optimism and playfulness, even through the most unthinkable of events.

Stephanie Becker, thirty, fell into the loving arms of Agawak sisters after the tragic death of her older brother, who committed suicide three weeks before camp began in June 2014.

"When I drove up to camp a week after his death, I got out of the car and just melted," recalls Stephanie. "I had tried to be so strong for my parents at home. At camp, the emotions came in a flood. No matter where I turned, there was somebody there to help me. Camp, being that sacred, safe, loving place, started to give me life again. Camp friends made me laugh again. Really, they ended up saving my life."

I heard the words "Camp saved my life" from many women who were met with more subtle forms of adversity. Some described being ostracized by the "cool girls" at school, and the newfound security of feeling total acceptance at camp. Others considered camp a much-needed thaw from chilly parents.

Tears well up in Gail Watkins's eyes when she

speaks about her summers at Echo Hill. "I remember during rest hour, our counselor Gracie Brown would read to us, and she would take turns stroking our heads and rubbing our backs," says Gail. "She was so kind. She made each of us in that cabin feel really loved. My parents both worked all the time; they owned a restaurant in Georgetown. They weren't the parents who would dote on us, even when they were home. At camp, I immediately felt like I was part of this large doting family."

I know well this sense of strangers becoming the tightest of families, built sturdily layer by layer, summer after summer, challenge by challenge, laugh by laugh.

As this camp girl evolved into a camp teen, and now a camp woman months from Medicare, I realize that this is perhaps the most fundamental lesson, an ability to adapt to communal living and form friendships with people far different than me. While nearly all of us were Jewish, our parental influences and personalities varied sharply. We learned inclusion decades before it became a cultural buzzword.

We had to—with one sink and one bathroom and seven beds inches away from each other, tiny house living forces you to get really cozy, really fast.

Yet we camp girls who grew up together in "our own little village," as Terry Worth calls it, are blessed with the absolute certainty that we can count on each other, however different we are.

We reminisce with regret that as children, we sometimes succumbed to a girl-gang mentality and shut someone out of our cliques. We talk about how some of our friends came to camp shortly after their parents' divorce, and how camp was a steady rudder, away from unsteady lives at school or at home.

I realized early on how lucky I was to have a solid home life once summer came to an end. I did not flee to camp as an escape.

My parents stayed married, and were demonstrative in their love for their children. We lived in the same house and I attended the same schools with the same friends until I went to college. Though I still consider camp to be my steadiest rudder—the one home I have been able to claim from age eight until now. Structured and stable, camp is the legato, the flowing and un-broken melody in a long life filled with staccato bursts.

After leaving my hometown of Oak Park, Illinois, I lived as a college student in California, as a fledgling reporter in Texas, as a newlywed in the District of Columbia, and as a mother raising four sons in Maryland.

Each state and each stage brings on a kaleidoscope of distinct memories.

I remember a Fleetwood Mac concert in Palo Alto and the penetrating voice of Stevie Nicks singing "Say You Love Me." Soon after, on my twenty-first birthday, I had a big fight with a boyfriend in front of the Pirates of the Caribbean ride at Disneyland. We stomped off and rode in separate cars. Pre–cell phones, it took me two hours to find him, at which time we continued our brawl, this while walking alongside a coosome couple with huge fixed smiles, giant Minnie and Mickey characters.

I remember the summer of 1980, anxiously flinging clothes on my bed in search of the right outfit to debut on my first day as the fashion writer at the *Dallas Times Herald*. I ultimately chose maroon ostrich cowboy boots, a flowered silk shirt, and a tiered blue jean skirt.

It was my first newspaper job, and I remember the thrill as I filed a story for the first time on a computer, rather than an IBM Selectric. It was about the Dallas Cowboys' new uniforms, which featured silver metallic stretch pants.

I remember how those glittery pants were emblematic of a spangled Dallas disco scene, which, combined with the unrelenting heat, ignited a sense of being very hot and happening. Some nights I even hung out with the Cowboys, as wide receiver Tony Hill, number 80, was a friend from college.

I remember entering a dark newsroom filled with cigarette smoke in Washington, DC, five years later on my first day as a reporter at United Press International, assigned to profile celebrities. It felt like I had landed on top of the world as I interviewed people like Yoko Ono, Betty Friedan, Annie Leibovitz, Ted Kennedy, and Queen Noor.

I had long red nails and a bulging Rolodex.

I remember so many names and faces: of controlling editors who made me a better writer and of uncontrolled journalism colleagues who introduced me to oyster shooters. I remember a great boyfriend who drove a Jeep and a creepy one who had slicked-back hair and would park in front of my apartment on nondate nights.

Many of these players that shaped me along the way have long disappeared, or are now relegated to the rank of Facebook friends with whom I have no off-line communication.

Memories of each important person who marks the passages of an evolving lifetime come unexpectedly, in episodic flashes and pieces, all fleeting.

The memories that last are from that March night in Chicago when I married Chuck, and my relief to have found this kind and patient man.

The memories that last are the birth of four sons that came in rapid succession, and raising babies into young men, in a house of shingles near the Chesapeake Bay.

The memories that last are of my departed parents, who still speak to me every day. In the kitchen, my mom gives me advice on how much cottage cheese to put in the kugel recipe, how long to cook a brisket.

Neither ever tastes as good as hers.

Today, I am poring through letters that my mother wrote to me at camp, in her elegant, familiar cursive, and I cannot stop the tears. Her voice is so loud and so present, the accent heavy. Instead of "Dear Iris," she would always start out "My Iya," using her nickname for me. And she always signed off with "I love you so much, and miss you so much. We're so happy for you that you are happy at camp."

The letters are long, three and four pages of swirly writing on diaphanous sheets of pale-green stationery, which I kept in their envelopes, the six-cent stamps intact.

She told me things I was too young and too busy swimming and laughing to understand: that she was bored and lonely, "counting the days until Visiting Weekend," that my dad worked long days, that she would go into our empty bedrooms and talk to us.

I wish I could tell her that I understand all of it

now, that I am her now, a mother with some arthritis who talks to empty bedrooms and misses the noise of children, their fights, their smells. I am the mother who is happy that her kids are happy and successful away from home, though I long for them in my quiet home.

Thank you, God, again and again, for Camp Agawak, for giving my mother uninterrupted stretches of time to sit down at the kitchen table alone and write letters to a daughter in a loving voice now immortalized.

She is still teaching me, thirteen years after her funeral, that as our children get strong on their own, mothers need to be even stronger on our own. She is teaching me to write letters to my kids, that the countless texts we exchange will eviscerate, that pen on paper sticks.

While my mother gave me lots of child-rearing advice, I also learned about raising children from learning to raise myself at camp, spurred on by others.

Members of my camp-girl tribe born of old Camp Agawak are now women who still play jacks together, cross-legged on the floor, though some have rebuilt hips and knees. And we now lace our reunions with margaritas and martinis, and not the Fizzies and Tang our parents used to send.

When I bring my everlasting girl circle to life with friends devoted to other camps, these strangers feel intensely familiar to them. Even if their own campgrounds occupied coasts far from the cheese-curd-and-bratwurst Midwest town of Minocqua, they know what I know and feel what I feel: Once a camper, always a camper.

Eyes light up as their own memories pour forth, rapid and loud, of canoe trips and Color Wars and soul-deep friendships that make all others pale. We are sisters from other mother ships, but who all consider camp and its communities to be part of our DNA. We are aging orphans who will never feel alone because we have our ageless camaraderie.

"Oh, the place that is cherished so deep in our hearts, where friendships are firm and true" begin the lyrics of another traditional Agawak song. I sang this softly to put four toddlers to bed and still sing this in the shower. That song makes me wistful not from sadness, but with a rush of gratitude that I

have these people and this place and a heart brimming with bottomless memories.

Camp girls are linked from youth until death do we part, though even in death we appear to be connected. Finding my camp friend Susie epitomizes this circle of life.

When I returned to Agawak the summer of 2014, I helped organize an on-premises alumni reunion weekend, a tradition entering its seventh year. The event was designed for childhood friends to leave their partners, cares, and makeup behind, pack sweats and sleeping bags, live in our old cabins, and swim, water-ski, and hike. Previously, all our reunions were held off-season at restaurants or hotels, to which we arrived in pretty clothes and mascara.

For the first couple of summer reunions, we located everyone but Susie, who had triceps at ten and whose prowess in sports was legendary. Susie was the best of the best in everything: the prize hitter in softball, the slammer in volleyball, the champion in swim races who barely took a breath, and voted the White Team captain. She had short black hair and dark brown eyes that were like lasers; those eyes did not look at you, they penetrated through you.

We worshipped her.

Susie was the daughter of a single mother, Ruth Wiedenbeck, the revered head counselor of Agawak, who began in 1965 and stayed on for twenty-one years.

We called Ruth "Big Weed" and Susie "Little Weed," abridged from their last name, and having nothing to do with the slang term for marijuana.

Every conversation and every email I received from my campmates as our alumni weekends approached always ended with "Find Little Weed!" No one had heard from Susie since our last day as campers in 1970.

She had left her hometown of Milwaukee right out of high school, bound for a college none of us could remember. She was not on social media and did not come up on Google. But Ruth Wiedenbeck did when I paired her name with their hometown of Milwaukee, and I discovered she had died in 1974, at the age of seventy-six.

Big Weed's obituary did not list a cause of death. However, it did say that she was survived by one daughter, Susan, who lived in Oregon. Just Oregon, not a specific city or town—just this one state.

Finding Susie reminded me of my earliest days in journalism when I would comb through fat phone books to locate people. This time, I spent hours picking my way through the online white pages, which finally led me to a listing in Linn County, 110 miles south of Portland.

There was an address with no phone number, and although it could have been another Susan Wiedenbeck, I knew it was her. The legendary athlete we feared on the playing fields, who carried the heaviest backpacks on our camping trips, would, of course, live in the woods. I imagined her camped out alone in a cabin, and I was not far wrong.

I wrote her a letter on Agawak stationery, telling her I was back working at camp and listing our friends who were planning to visit for a reunion weekend. I told her that she had to join us and gave my email and phone number. The letter was mailed on a Monday; I got a call that Thursday.

As soon as I said, "Hello, it's Iris," she gasped and got weepy, a jag of tears so unexpected from this girl of steel. She was a forest ranger. She had just broken up with her partner. She would be there for the reunion. Her voice gave me chills— so much like her raspy-voiced mother.

Susie said she had thought about Agawak often since her last year as a camper, and she knew she would return someday. She had to, she said; it was her mother's wish—she would explain. As soon as we hung up, this email went out to my Agawak women: "I found Susie! A missing link in our chain of history."

Susie was the first to arrive at camp that summer, saddled with a steel-framed backpack. She was wearing baggy athletic shorts and a faded T-shirt. Her graying hair was still short, and those eyes, those eyes, were still lasers.

Susie was back!

It was an hour before the rest of our gang would arrive, and Susie and I sat on a bottom bunk in Cabin 12 and shared highlights of the past forty-seven years. I told her about my husband and our four sons. She told me about how she fell apart when "Mama died," and how she had recently endured the death of a long romantic relationship.

Susie whispered: "I was happiest here. We loved each other without judgment."

She then revealed that it was not only her friends and the camp that had drawn her back: Her mother had been cremated, and one of her requests was to have some of her ashes scattered in Blue Lake.

Susie unzipped a side pocket of her pack and pulled out what would become known that weekend as "a bag of Weed." Yes, some of Ruth Wiedenbeck's ashes were in a large plastic Ziploc.

When the rest of the group arrived, we sat on the splintery wooden floor of the cabin in a circle, like we had so many summers as children. Lots was different though; instead of sharing Smarties and Pez, we were sharing a wedge of brie and a gallon of vodka.

As the newcomer to our July reunions, Susie was the focus of our conversation, the star of the night. We wanted to know everything about the last years of Big Weed's life—our head counselor who had a gap in her front teeth and would put two fingers in her mouth and let out a shrill whistle heard all over camp. If that whistle was followed by a barky bellow of your name, you stopped cold, because you knew you were in trouble.

Susie relayed that her mother, a physical education teacher during the school year, had felt the most joy and a sense of belonging at camp. As her daughter put it: "She *lived* for camp." Thus the importance of making sure that she would always be a part of this place, in the form of strewn ashes.

We asked Agawak's director of waterskiing, Bill Fuhrmann, to take us out on a sunset cruise. With an ice chest on board, we would head for the cove where we used to ride our horses in the water.

The cruise began with hilarity, then fell into a somber silence as Bill glided the pontoon slowly to our desired spot. We had dressed in camp uniforms, white shirts and navy shorts or jeans, to honor Big Weed's final pilgrimage.

As the boat idled in the cove, we each grabbed a fistful from the Ziploc bag. While most of us had buried one or both of our parents, none of us had ever touched human remains. It felt scary and exciting and surreal. We kept our hands tightly clenched until it was our turn to toss, which we had decided would be accompanied by each of us saying something we loved about our head counselor.

While throwing out her round of ashes, Jill Hirschfield said she loved the head counselor's whistle. Another woman shared that Big Weed was often more maternal and caring than their own mothers were. Susie teared up when she added that with us, on that lake, was the best she had felt in a very long time, embraced by a rich history and a renewed closeness to her mom.

I talked about how I had always wanted to please Big Weed, to earn her praise, and that in doing so, I became my best self. She would always say that to be good enough is not enough, that we should always try to be great.

After my farewell toast, I opened my palm and saw a one-inch piece of bone lodged in the ashes. I wanted to scream, but as not to disrupt the serenity, I quickly emptied my hand over the side of the boat. Only instead of landing in the lake, the bone landed in my martini.

I could not help but laugh as I told the group there was a bone in my drink. Susie laughed, too, and said that whatever they do in the process of cremation it was clear her mom was too tough to completely dissolve into dust.

Subdued on beverages and the dusty-peach sunset, we talked about how it was our Agawak sisters who had held us up while weathering the losses in our lives.

We are there for cancer survivors, survivors of deaths in the family, survivors of the deaths of marriages. We are there for Little Weed, to laugh and cry over the ashes that left a temporary char in our palms but marked a ceremony that honored the length and depth of our friendships.

On that boat, we were reminded that we are all, forever, part of Agawak and Big Weed, and her yellow Clairol hair, which she wore in a Beatles cut. This sentiment was further immortalized when, with one hand clutching the now-empty plastic bag, Susie put two fingers from her other hand into her mouth and let out a loud and piercing whistle—her mother's whistle.

We then locked hands and softly sang "Taps":

"Day is done, gone the sun, from the lakes, from the hills, from the skies. All is well. Safely rest. God is nigh." This is the song we sang to end every campfire, the song we sang decades later to ease our babies to sleep. This is the song that the bugle plays at military memorials and was a lights-out signal to soldiers as far back as the Civil War.

This iconic centuries-old song echoes within as we leave each other at the end of our weekend reunion. It reminds us that we will always find a way back to each other, even when one of us is living alone in the woods without email.

We may make new friends, but the old friends are the pillars. *"One is silver, and the other is gold,"* as the lyric goes in the song "Friends"—sung by campers everywhere.

We never did lose the old, this gang that giggled and gabbed on our beds with flashlights when we were supposed to be asleep. We stood next to each other as teens in front of the bathroom mirror, securing soup cans to our heads after slathering our hair with Dippity-Do to straighten out the curls.

We sobbed together the last night of camp as

we sat on the beach watching our handcrafted birch-bark boats, aflame with candles, float away on Blue Lake, dreading the next day that would separate us.

My camp sisters spent a lot of time with a man that my husband and four children never got to meet. All of my Agawak friends knew my father, and they bring him to life again for me with stories of his generosity.

They recall the gifts he used to bring for every girl in our cabin on Parents' Weekend. In 1968, he brought red baseball hats imprinted with BORN TO BE WILD, the title of Steppenwolf's hit release of that year. I am saddened by that recollection, realizing what I did not realize then: He was one hip dad.

The photographs of my father I now have everywhere in the house are lifeless and flat. Agawak friends bring him out of the frames and place them next to me, alive and loving. Margie Gordon remembers that when my dad was watching me go over a jump on a horse during Parents' Weekend, he said, "That's my girl."

I hear these stories, and he is next to me again:

so tall, with kind brown eyes, always with an arm around my shoulders.

I am remembering that when I was in dark, sad moods, he would instruct me to go into the bathroom, look into the mirror, and say "I'm great, I'm great" one hundred times. I could never get through the first twenty without breaking out in laughter. He made me feel great when I felt awful, and still does when I think of this little girl in the bathroom talking to a mirror.

Throughout my life, my dad would say "That's my girl" following any accomplishment, big or small. He said it when I won a community spelling bee in fourth grade. I heard those words for the last time when I snagged my interview with Queen Noor, held in the palace in Amman, Jordan, just weeks before he died.

Yet his words never die, and keep propelling me onward. His two favorite sayings were "You gotta swing with it" and "Kick open a new door."

When I first heard the swing-with-it advice, I asked him, "Swing with what?" He said, "Swing with everything. You will have a lot of hard things to get through as you get older. And you gotta swing with them all."

Long after his simple pine coffin was lowered into the frozen ground on a February afternoon in Chicago, I have swung through the loss of both parents, rejection letters, bad flights, bad fights with teenage sons, bad wrinkles. I know from a father's voice that will never be silenced that we have to swing with hard things or those hard swings will knock us down.

I also know that when I am down the camp girls are there to pick me up, to make me laugh, to remind me "I'm great, I'm great."

We will swing with it, together, through the good and the bad, until death do us part, a vow that may not have come to fruition with some of our marriages but will always be a camp-girl promise we keep.

We camp friends may have gray hair now, but because of each other, we will forever have teenage hearts.

Chapter Three
Ambition

"Pushing through fear as children turns into fearless-ness as we carry on, as every step to and through adulthood is competitive and hard."

I am on my usual walk on the Baltimore & Annapolis Trail, through a pastoral stretch of fields filled with peonies and sunflowers. My camp friend Liz Weinstein is on her usual walk in Glencoe, Illinois, on the Green Bay Trail, bordered by train tracks and a canopy of oak trees and maples.

We like to talk on the phone while we are huffing 750 miles apart, singing the songs we sang on our hikes long ago. On this morning, we are belting out *"Oh, what a beautiful morning, oh, what a beautiful day,"* from *Oklahoma*, a production we staged at Agawak in 1967.

When we get to this line, we draw it out and scream in unison: "I've got a beeeeuuutccefulll feeling. Everything's going my way."

When talking to a camp girl, I always feel like everything is going my way.

I ask Liz how many miles she generally walks. She says, "Four," and I instantly feel the fire of competition from my camper days. I do only three. The following week as I am panting near the four-mile mark, I call Liz and sing this line from *Annie Get Your Gun*: "I can do anything better than you."

That night, we talk on the phone about how this instinctive urge to be the best, this undying competitive streak, was primed at camp. Whatever we played, we played to win, whether to top our last performances or to topple the other team in Blue and White games. The quality of ambition that we gained at camp was fierce and constant—and has stuck for a lifetime.

Our drive was at its most extreme when the teams faced off in Capture the Flag, the most adrenaline-pumping and points-bearing of all our competitions.

Capture the Flag meant everything at the time, and it remains a capstone Agawak game. During our camper years, it was the season's biggest competition between the Blue Team and the White Team, the culmination of dozens of lesser-point games that had taken place over the past weeks. The team that emerged victorious at summer's end got a large silver trophy and an immeasurable burst of gratification.

It was played at night, with limited use of flashlights, making this competition also the most injury-producing. Capture the Flag inevitably resulted in lots of bruises and sprains, and sometimes a few breaks.

The game begins with a long whistle, then the two teams crisscross en masse and charge through enemy territory with the goal to grab the other team's flag. The collective screams, which sound like the high-pitched cries of red foxes, combined with the velocity of a full-on assault of bodies, always reminds me of soldiers with bayonets charging on horses.

The roots of Capture the Flag actually do harken back to battles between soldiers on foot and on horseback, who knew the outcome once a flag was taken. The job assigned to the color guards during the Civil War was to protect their flag, and they often risked their lives to ward off the enemy.

And like those battles, then and now, Capture the Flag at Agawak can get ugly. We turn from one family into divided warriors. In her best-selling book *A Mindfulness Guide for the Frazzled*, comedian and talk show host Ruby Wax took sarcastic aim at the intensity of team games she played as an Agawak girl in the 1960s. As she wrote: "It was called Camp Agawak, which probably means 'go for the jugular...' and the message was: Beat the opposition at all costs! Conquer! Conquer! Conquer!"

The name Agawak has no hidden meaning, other than it is our brother camp Kawaga spelled backward. The will to conquer *was* very real, and it did take its toll.

In my camper days, one flag was on the top of a steep hill, the other on the bottom. Tripping over gnarled roots in the dark and on steep inclines resulted in so many injuries that in recent years the location was switched to a flat expanse of grassy field that is still used. The nursing staff is now parked on the sidelines.

Getting the flag takes a swift dive into the dirt, dodging several pairs of the guards' firmly planted feet. By the time a flag is captured—a process that can take several hours—there are only a few players left on the field. Because if you are tagged by an opponent, you are immobilized in a roped area called "jail."

It is the final night of our alumni reunion, and we are standing around a bonfire. As inevitably happens when the group is together, we start reminiscing about which team won the team trophies in years past and who lost Capture the Flag.

I feel again the pain searing through my head that I felt when I was twelve. A burly older camper did not just tag me out; she tackled me out when my outstretched hand was three inches away from grabbing the White Team flag. The force of that tackle hurled me to the ground and gave me a large bump on the right side of my nose.

The fire has turned into glowing embers, and we are holding hands that are sticky from the marshmallows we pulled off our sticks to make s'mores. We decide to go around and each share a lingering memory from our camper days.

Flashbacks of the ferocity of team games, particularly Capture the Flag, come up immediately from nearly off of us. We will never get over the urgency and passion of that game. We will never get over the big wins and big losses at camp that remain fresh in our aging minds. I have a ridge on my nose more than fifty years later that makes it impossible for me to ever forget.

Liz Weinstein and I stay behind to gather a bucket of lake water to douse the last of the fire. We are silent in the familiar hiss and smoke that ended all of our campfires for so many summers. Sitting on a wooden bench near Cabin 15, where we lived with these friends as teens, we talk about how Capture the Flag has become a metaphor for how we have steered our lives, knowing the value of hard work and teamwork with an eye on the prize.

"In that game, you had to give one hundred percent one hundred percent of the time," says Liz, owner of a graphic design firm, a former Blue Team captain, and one of only twenty campers in Agawak history to earn the most advanced level in swimming, a purple cap.

"I've channeled the spirit of Capture the Flag all of my life, as I have built a team in my company, faced fierce competition, and avoided getting tagged out," she adds.

Competitiveness driven by tenacity, focus, and ambition is the foundation for success in team games at camp. Long after camp girls become camp women, these qualities become the drivers of a successful life. We climb relentlessly for the prize in our careers; we search for prize relationships.

Susan Green, sixty, was captain of the White Team and a three-time Olympic Day queen, and joined

Liz in the small group of purple caps. She is now a senior vice president and partner of a major Wall Street wealth management firm. She says her formidable career has its roots in the drive developed during her summers at camp.

"The personal and professional choices I have made are directly related to the confidence I received from my achievements at camp," says Susan. "This gave me the ability to develop a belief system that I could do anything I wanted if I set goals and worked hard to achieve them.

"Then working as a team in games like softball, volleyball, and Capture the Flag become critical building blocks as you enter adulthood and become team players and leaders in professions," she continues. "Like high-jumping, once you clear a certain goal, you raise the bar and work hard to clear that next height. We certainly learned this at camp."

When we discuss our present-day achievements and the challenges we faced to get over subsequent bars, talk swerves to the old days. While Capture the Flag was the most coveted game to win, another competition that gets us riled in reverie is the race across the lake between the Blue and White war canoes. Ten paddlers from each team started off together in the middle of the lake in twelve-foot green wooden boats. Today, the camp war canoes are nearly twice as long, hold twenty-two, and are fiberglass.

The boats are steered by a coxswain at the stern, who synchronizes the plowing arms with repetitive shouts of: "Stroke up, stroke up, stroke up!" The war-canoe showdown results in two beachfront huddles, one exalted, one sunken, and both sides with muscles that burn for days.

When I was fourteen, in the second-oldest cabin, the war-canoe race took place on a fifty-four-degree afternoon under leaden skies and pellets of rain. My Blue Team was ahead by the length of two boats from the start until nearly the finish line, which was the outer rope that penned in the swimming area. We were three yards from the end when the White Team shot past us, and with shrieks that rivaled those of howler monkeys, held up their paddles in a victory salute.

As their paddles shot up, our heads fell into our laps.

I have thought of that cold, disappointing day on other cold, disappointing days over the past fifty years. Two important lessons came from that dismal scene, when I watched the winners in their circle of joy from our circle of doom.

For one, although I had been on the losing team throughout many past summers of competition, the magnitude of this loss, an unexpected split-second fall from first place, really hammered home the value of bucking up and being a gracious loser.

Our team captain spoke about sportsmanship, and how we would face lots of other losses at camp. "No one likes a sore loser. Let's wipe our tears and congratulate the other team," she instructed, then shepherded us over to the celebrating champions.

I cannot say that the sting of loss was ever completely eradicated after a big game at camp, even with a show of grace. But I can say when the scoreboard tipped our way, it helped us all become humbler winners, knowing too well the pain of being beaten.

I also learned to never again be overly confident. With the sustained lead of the Blue canoe, we assumed we had snagged the race, so the power of our paddles slackened as the finish line was only strokes away. Those of us who occupied those old wooden boats can laugh today about our crying jags after losing war-canoe competitions. We can laugh about our steadfast obsession with other Blue and White games, which were so close, were surely ours, then eluded our grasp in a surprise finish.

Lots of sleepaway camps have Color Wars, though the competition is often played over one grueling week, and the team affiliation for campers changes every season. At Agawak, we play games all summer, and the team we are designated remains our team for life.

A new Agawak camper is assigned a team color during the second day of the season. Up until 1980, at the beginning of camp the new girls picked their teams from a hat filled with crumpled pieces of paper marked blue or white. This tradition has since shifted in creative directions, like handing each new camper a cupcake with blue or white filling, revealed after the first bites.

Whether the games last one week or the two-month season, team competition is an impassioned and unforgettable camp tradition. When I began an interview with Leni Landorf, an Agawak girl in the 1940s, her first question to me was: "Were you a Blue or a White?" I told her I was Blue, and she began singing her White Team fight song, which is still sung today: *When a White Team girl walks down the street, she's got that one hundred percent, from head to feet. She has a word, a smile, a winning way…*"

Our tradition of being a Blue or a White for a lifetime makes team loyalty run deep into adulthood, ridiculous as it seems This is serious stuff because once a Blue or a White, always a Blue or White.

Those games we played that gave us the highest of highs and the lowest of lows are part of the toolbox that prepared us for handling everything we do now.

The competition, which could turn very rough, was frightening to us as youngsters. But pushing through fear turns into fearlessness as we carry on, as every step to and through adulthood is competitive and hard.

I recall my terror as a nine-year-old when the

Blue Team captain, a position granted by election, mapped out our Capture the Flag strategy. As sixty girls, then half the camp, sat on the floor of the library, which served as the Blue headquarters, she stood in front of us, holding a clipboard, and thundered our orders: "Run like racehorses and charge for the White flag, no matter what it takes."

We learned quickly that it takes a lot. Some of the most docile girls could turn savage, so as not to disappoint their teammates and captain.

In 1970, I was that teenager standing in front of the Blue Team as captain, an honor I still revere as one of the peaks of this long life. Seriously. Only a camp girl would understand how much this meant. I talked so often to my kids about my captain year, how I felt like royalty, that when they introduce me to friends they still sometimes say: "Our mom is a writer, and she was the Blue Team captain."

When I was explaining strategy for Capture the Flag, remembering my own fright at a captain's orders, I told the girls: "We can win this" and not "We have to win this." I knelt down in front of the youngest campers and said: "If you do not want to play, you do not have to."

No one bowed out, and we won the game, because of a tiny but speedy ten-year-old who wedged herself between a big girl's legs and snatched the White Team banner.

After that victory, I wrote this in my letter home:

Dear Mom and Dad, We captured the flag, and the Blues will probably win the trophy! That game lasted for hours, and I can barely walk now. But willpower beat exhaustion!

I read that now and think of all the times in subsequent decades that my willpower beat out exhaustion. During Capture the Flag, we run so hard our lungs burst in icy agony—and yet we keep going. Our legs are searing—and we keep going. Sometimes we win. Sometimes we lose. Yet we never stop trying.

I know how the hard-earned flag of the opponent felt in my hands when I finally did grab it one game a lifetime ago. I know that it pays to be a humble victor, and not boastful. I know that defeat means you stand tall, congratulate the winners, and fight harder the next time around.

A show of grace with both victory and defeat are necessary character traits to succeed at summer camp, tempering ambition with empathy and humility. These lessons are crucial in a community where competitive games go on all summer.

The four biggest honors at camp, which overshadowed all others, were to earn a purple Cap, to be crowned Olympic Queen, to be named All-Around Camper, and to be elected a team captain. My alumni pals Liz Weinstein and Susan Green were each bestowed with all four of these coveted titles, and they both count these events as some of the most thrilling of their lives.

I see now, though, that in our camper days perhaps too much of our focus was on beating out the other team, or on beating out the other person, to land first prize. Because decades later, I found out that camp winners do not always feel like winners. I was surprised to find out that one of my dearest camp friends did not feel the power and pride many do after getting voted captain by her whole team.

Peggy Gilbert was the stunning and popular daughter of the former director of Agawak. She became captain of the White Team the year I was at the helm of the Blues. Just recently, she told me, "I made myself throw up all that summer." Peggy and I had been cabinmates since we were ten, and I would never have imagined she was racked with a faltering self-image that led to an eating disorder.

Like gaining the "freshman 15" in college, it was easy to pack on the weight at camp, with family-style servings in large bowls, refilled with seconds and thirds. Peggy reminded me how painfully aware we all were of how much we would gain, as we had to get on the scale every Saturday during weekly weigh-in at the infirmary, a policy shelved long ago. We also changed clothes five times a day, and could not help but check each other out, seeing tighter bodies and better curves that could make us feel fat and inferior.

Peggy's fight with food lasted decades, and the

struggles she surmounted put her on the path to becoming a licensed clinical social worker and addiction counselor. She now works as the director of education at a nonprofit organization that provides programs and resources on depression awareness and suicide prevention for middle and high school students.

With her professional expertise and personal plight, Peggy was also tapped by the Foundation for Jewish Camp to contribute to a manual for training camp staff to work with the growing number of campers struggling with mental health issues.

Here is a small excerpt from Peggy's portion of the manual, which advises camp counselors to speak openly with their campers about anxieties and fears.

> *I remember my last summer as a camper, when I was fifteen and captain of the White Team, something all the girls in the highest cabin wanted to be. I spent most of that summer in the bathroom secretly vomiting away my fears of not being good enough.*

By identifying what you see and expressing your concern, you send the message that there is a different and healthier way to deal with life's pressures. You have these girls for a relatively short time over the summer, but you have enormous power to make a difference in their lives.

I have talked to Peggy often lately to learn of her progress as she recovers from cancer. We have long conversations about our work and our kids and always about camp, the good and the bad. One bad memory is how we would starve ourselves for a day before our weekly weigh-ins. We regret that we equated skinny with pretty.

I told Peggy I had no idea she was suffering— she was the White Team captain, after all—and here is her response:

PEGGY

Oh, yeah, there were many insecurities. I actually got instructions on how to throw up from another girl in our cabin. I lived in a dual world. I was a camp leader, and on the outside maybe everything about me looked happy and perfect. But there is this underbelly to life, right? My internal world said I wasn't good enough. I developed an eating disorder to fill a void. And this went on for years.

At camp, everyone seemed confident all the time, and there were times that I didn't. At home, I would look at my beautiful mother, who herself never thought she was thin enough, and I would always feel huge, even at a normal weight.

It took a lot of therapy to get into a place where I was more self-accepting. Back in the 1970s, when we were fifteen and struggling with our self-images, we didn't have a name for what I was going through and we certainly didn't talk about it. I needed help, but there was no structure in place to recognize I needed help.

Many young kids come to camp today on medication, with psychiatric histories, and there is an understanding now that those issues are real and that camps must be equipped to deal with them.

While I was studying at the University of Chicago to become a social worker in 1981, Time *magazine did a cover story on eating disorders, and Jane Fonda was featured as she shared the story of her struggle with bulimia. Suddenly I had a name for my destructive behavior. I sought out one of the doctors featured in the article for help, and my recovery began.*

Body image issues are often generational and can be hard to shake. Even today, I worry about the inevitable weight gain that comes with the medication I am on that will help prolong my life. At least today I recognize how crazy that thinking is.

We worry so much about superficial things when we are teenagers, like how to fit in with the cool girls, who seem prettier and better. As adults, we have deeper things to worry about, and it is then that we understand what really matters.

As Peggy describes, there is now pervasive awareness of how "not feeling good enough" can take its toll on teens grappling with self-identity. This, in a world that is far more stressful and competitive than the one we faced. More camps are adding professionals to support camper and staff emotional and social health. At Agawak, there are persons who oversee cabin life for each of the age divisions, Junior, Intermediate, and Senior.

When cabin conflicts occur, they sit with that group and they talk it out. Girls with unhealthy dietary habits are sent for supervision to camp nurses, who are also in charge of dispensing medications, which grow in volume every summer, according to people I spoke to representing a variety of camps.

"Children are more stressed than ever, and are expected to have high performance in every facet of their lives," says Keala Strahan, the head nurse at Camp Matoaka in Smithfield, Maine. "I am definitely seeing an increase in younger and younger kids being placed on antidepressant medications, as well as medications for the treatment of ADHD and ADD.

"As the campers get older and learn appropriate coping mechanisms to better self-regulate their symptoms, I strongly encourage parents to discuss a drug holiday with their physicians as an option for summer, when kids aren't expected to perform on demand," continues Keala. "This, as long as their medication is not one they have to take every day to maintain its efficacy in their system. I've seen positive effects of these no-drug summers, as camp allows for more learning through play, imagination, and creative thinking."

* * *

I have also witnessed how competition in a camp setting, away from the intense pressure of academics, can be a positive force in strengthening character in a place where kids learn by experience and not on demand.

Both of Keala's daughters were Matoaka campers and Color War captains, and have served as counselors there. As a mother who watched her girls mature and toughen from camp competition, like I did with my boys, Keala reinforces the sentiment that working hard for a win at camp can be the scaffolding for a winning adulthood, and that ambition is a good thing, if kept in check.

"Camp kids learn at a young age that someone wins and someone loses, and that's life," says Keala. "Team competition has been fundamental in shaping our girls. Wanting to win has set the foundation for them to be driven to succeed, to learn that it's okay to be determined—not to be ruthless, but to be strong.

"Children growing up today will vie for positions in a very competitive society, and it's good to be ambitious," she adds. "No matter what facet of life you are dealing with, in college or in jobs or in relationships, wanting to win forces you to dig down and find courage within yourself that's going to carry you throughout your life."

At summer camp, we do learn that anything worth having is worth fighting for, and that we can never win it all. This knowledge has been an indomitable force that has softened my response to failure and fortified my determination to succeed.

I have heard from my college students who did not go to camp that coming of age as competitive female athletes in high school and college— something my generation of women was unable to do—can instill the same sense of tenacity and drive. I, too, have found that pushing myself hard physically helps fan my mental fortitude to keep climbing the rungs in a long career.

My first job out of college was in a drab brick building next to the glass-and-steel John Hancock Building, where the coolest public relations firm in Chicago was housed. The Hancock Building, which sparkled in the sun, was like the White Team's flag, beckoning me to capture it. I wanted in to this firm that handled publicity for the best restaurants, stores, theaters, and rock-and-roll venues. I wanted out of my windowless office, where I was the account executive for a retirement home, and where colleagues chain-smoked and wore glum expressions.

Unfailingly, surly bosses would make assignments near the end of the day, press releases to be completed on deadline before work ended at 5 p.m. This, just as I was applying my Revlon red lipstick and prepping to escape to the singles bars a few blocks away, on Division Street.

I was the lowliest staff member, and therefore a servant. My dad, who started at the bottom and worked his way to the top, would tell me to put a smile on my face and do whatever I was asked to do, that this would pay off.

It was dreadful work, and I got a pit in my stomach every morning as I boarded the northbound 151 bus on Michigan Avenue, en route to a job for which I earned $150 a week. But I listened to my father, did my best, fattened my media contacts, and sharpened my writing skills.

Six months later, I got an interview for an account executive/writer position at my dream firm in the incandescent Hancock tower next door. I wore a black suit and pearl earrings and channeled the camp-girl spirit: Believe in yourself. You can do this.

When I was asked about my writing experience, I said I had churned out dozens of press releases at my current job, had written for my college newspaper, and had been a published author since the age of eight at Camp Agawak. Turns out Susan, the daughter of the boss of the agency, Margie Korshak, was also an Agawak girl.

Like so many other times in life, camp karma served as a guiding angel on my shoulder. In this case, I conducted a confident interview, solidified by my writing ability and helped by my Agawak connection. I got the job, and my four years with the Korshak agency gave me some rip-roaring twenties.

I moved from promoting the retirement home into dazzling new places and accounts: supervising publicity for Arnie Morton's restaurants, which included the launch of the very first Morton's, and for Park West, Chicago's premier entertainment venue.

I had my own office, on the thirtieth floor, with a wall of windows and a swooping view of Lake Michigan. From my perch on top of the town, I typed out press releases and dreamed of other jobs to capture. My work in public relations introduced me to top Chicago newspaper editors, who came to know my writing and would go on to hire me as they moved upward in their own careers.

When the sports editor of the *Chicago Daily News* moved to the *Dallas Times Herald* to become managing editor, he recruited me to be the paper's fashion writer. Four years later, when the executive editor of the *Chicago Tribune* became the executive editor of United Press International, he tapped me to become the wire service's national features writer, based in Washington, DC.

The will to capture the best assignments, the best interviews, is something I feel every day as a journalist. Like a young girl at camp, I keep forging onward when a goal eludes me, propelled by irrepressible willpower to keep on trying.

It took me three years to get an interview with Senator Ted Kennedy. He was my top pick to be the first in a series of five-thousand-word profiles

I was assigned to do for UPI, spotlighting writers, actors, artists, and politicians. This was 1984, long before a reporter could dash off a text or an email for an interview request. It was the era of pleading over a landline in fast-talk, before people had the chance to hang up on you.

Melody Miller was Kennedy's deputy press secretary, and during my initial ask, she did not say yes and she did not say no. She told me that the senator, then spearheading a push for expanded healthcare legislation, did not have time currently for an hour sit-down interview and to call back in a month.

I called back in a month to the day. Melody did not say yes and she did not say no. Again, she deferred a confirmation due to his hectic schedule and instructed me to call back in a month. Which I did, and did again, and did again—for almost three years.

During the months that she did not say yes and did not say no, I acted on a maybe. Maybe I will win and maybe I will lose, but I will stay in the game, like at camp, and keep playing with all of my might.

In November 1987, I made my monthly call on a Tuesday. Melody told me to come to Kennedy's office in the Russell Senate Office Building that Thursday. Despite the short notice, I was quite prepared with interview questions, having accumulated mounting research on his political rise while anticipating that the yes would eventually come. Camp had turned me into an adult who always worked my hardest toward the yes.

I got a lot of nos to get to this place.

The lasting influence that being a team captain had on me seems just as strong on campers today. When the Blues won the trophy at the end of the 2017 season, after several summers of losing, I shared with their captain, Olivia Baker, how lessons learned on camp playing fields had paved my adulthood with tenacity and endurance.

Olivia, then sixteen and a camper for a decade, told me that she had already experienced how team games had instilled the qualities I described. She was among the top achievers in her high school class, serving as the editor of the school paper, and had just learned of her acceptance to Columbia University.

She laughed at how her friends at home say things like, "Oh my God, your Blue and White competition sounds so crazy. It's like Viking warfare!"

Olivia then elaborated on how the long tentacles of camp girls' fighting spirit become even more expansive long after summer ends. "When I'm struggling with my studies or in anything I do, I always think about how I used my whole might to lead a team to victory in Capture the Flag," said Olivia. "And now, literally, I believe I can do anything. I feel like I can capture the job I want, the friends I want, and eventually the spouse I want."

My sons also know from their own competitive camper days that giving it their all is the ticket to every capture in life. Now in their twenties, they are maneuvering their way upward in the fields of filmmaking, technology, acting, and writing. They know that they can capture the prize only with grit and determination. They were reminded of this every day growing up in our house by an extraordinary athlete from nearby Baltimore.

There is a large poster that hangs in the hallway between their bedrooms, bearing a photograph of baseball legend Cal Ripken Jr. Above his picture is one word in large black letters: PERSEVERANCE.

Ripken holds the record in baseball for consistently showing up for work. He played 2,632 consecutive games with the Baltimore Orioles, spread out over more than sixteen years. He persevered through sickness and injuries and bad weather and still put on his uniform and came to work.

I tell my friend Liz Weinstein about the Ripken poster, and she shivers as it brings up this memory:

It is the last week of camp and it is raining—not hard, but not a drizzle. She is trying to pass her front-flip, half-twist jackknife dive, the last of ten dives she needs to achieve her purple cap, a goal she has been trying to reach for years. The judge is Beaver, the nickname for our critical waterfront director whose real name was Beverly. (I doubt we would call her Beaver if she were alive today.)

In order to pass, Liz has to do the final dive perfectly six consecutive times.

The completion of the task came on the twenty-third dive of the day, after an hour of climbing out of the cold lake into the cold air and after five summers of trying to go from a yellow cap to perfect purple.

"I can still hear Beaver saying 'Pass' as she checked off that dive on her clipboard," Liz says.

And I can still feel that captured white flag in my hands.

Chapter Four
Versatility

"As much as I loved hypersonic volleyball and tennis matches, some of my happiest memories are from when we were just lying on our beds and talking."

I am kayaking on the Severn River, which fronts the home where we have lived for going on thirty years. It is a sixty-two-degree April day, and I am drifting through the water, lying back in the seat, and drinking in the sun. I suddenly hear the words "You're lily-dipping!"

No one is talking. It is my memory rising in

a haunting chorus of the dozens of co-paddlers who have joined me in kayaks and canoes in team competitions and on camping trips. It's a phrase Agawak girls used to say, which means "You need to pull deeper, harder, faster!" and it comes from the image of only skimming Blue Lake's surface, where water lilies float like billowy angels.

Suddenly, as if the deciding points in the Blue-White Senior Swim Meet rest on me winning the kayak race, I bolt up straight, and go from a saunter to a sprint, in sync with an imaginary rapid-fire bark: "Stroke up, stroke up, stroke up!"

After my leisurely afternoon of kayaking turned into a frantic dash for a mental finish line, I am curious whether "lily-dipping" is a real word. It comes up in the Urban Dictionary, defined as "lacking intensity, adequacy, completeness."

Well, I can tell you this for certain: While there are inevitable waves of inadequacy that stream throughout the life cycle, at our core, and overall, no grown camp girl I know lacks intensity. Seasoned by full-throttle summers that teach us a bounty of skills, we become resourceful and adventurous adults who feel like we can do just about anything—no matter our age.

Or most anything.

I cannot do trapeze artistry and try out for Cirque du Soleil, as circus activities were not, and are not, featured at Agawak, as they are at some sleepaway camps. But I can still do the splits and a front flip on the trampoline.

We may have lapsed into lily-dipping as young campers a lifetime ago, in boats and in feigning sickness at the infirmary to avoid swimming on frigid days. In adulthood, we are navigating multifaceted lives, with unending curiosity. This because we were required to constantly try new things at camp, imprinting versatility and open-mindedness.

Leslie Jacobs, sixty, exemplifies how spending summers in a place where we worked all parts of ourselves, artistic, creative, and physical, can be the fuel for a long-distance ride. Leslie attended Camp O-Tahn-Agon in Three Lakes, Wisconsin, for seven seasons, starting at the age of seven. She calls those summers, sleeping in musty cabins and spinning from activity to activity, "the most grounding, confidence-building times of my life."

I tell Leslie how those confidence builders of the past continue to ground and exhilarate me. It can come from something as simple as walking next to the pine trees that line my driveway and remembering a walk through the forest at camp.

A four-season outdoorswoman who lives on a farm on a river in rural Indiana, Leslie says that "everything" in her world of woods and fields and water reminds her of camp, and continues to inspire her.

"I keep imagining that ten-year-old girl mastering tremendous skills like guiding one of those old, heavy wooden canoes through Level Three rapids, flipping the canoe, righting it, getting all the water out, and portaging to a campsite a mile away," says Leslie. "Or building a sturdy and long-lasting fire, sometimes with wet wood. Or swimming a mile to an island.

"And there were moments of just being still that I loved. We had a nondenominational service held on Sundays, near a rustic sign that said 'I come here to find myself; it's so easy to get lost in the world,' a John Burroughs quote. We would sing camp songs that perpetuated the notion that we could find peace and loving relationships in nature."

Her words throw me back to our campfires and stillness, where we did truly find ourselves, in singing songs of friendship and loyalty, and in the depth of peace and beauty found amid our birch and pine trees.

My shoulders also ache at her portaging story, as I recall a weeklong canoe trip through the Boundary Waters of Canada. Much of our voyage was spent in a torrent of rain, arms shaking from the weight of our green wooden canoes, in portages that were steep and long. That adventure was the most grueling experience of my then fourteen years, and like Leslie, something I look back on with great satisfaction. Being able to flex our physical prowess was something new for us.

For girls who started summer camp in the 1960s, years before the passage of Title IX prohibiting sex discrimination in education programs, most every athletic endeavor beyond kickball and Ping-

Pong was something new. Our school gym programs did not include training in rigorous sports like those offered to the boys.

I am flashing back to scenes from second grade, wistfully watching the boys' T-ball practices from the sidelines and dreading my ballet lessons, with the tight shoes and the teacher Miss Rose, who would tap our legs with a long stick.

While I played the forward position on a high school basketball team, half-court and barely breaking a sweat, the varsity boys were driving full-court presses, soaking through their uniforms of orange and blue, the colors of Oak Park–River Forest High School.

Spending eight weeks at Agawak for several summers, learning a variety of land and water sports, campers became capable and versatile athletes. Going to our activities was required, and we learned how to do it all: jump a horse, golf, fence, play softball and volleyball, pitch tents, build fires, shoot a bow and arrow and a rifle. On Blue Lake, I learned eight swimming strokes, six dives, and how to sail, canoe, row, kayak, and water-ski.

I can still glide through the water with the breaststroke I perfected at age ten, get up on a slalom ski, slam a volleyball serve, and jump a horse. And with the right pitch, I can hit a home run.

Leni Landorf, the Agawak camper in the 1940s, exemplifies just how deeply rooted are those skills and the psychic satisfaction that give camp girls an everlasting sense of competence. She traveled on an overnight train from her hometown of Cleveland to begin the first of six summers at Agawak.

Leni scoffs when I ask about her age. "I don't live my life by a number," she says. "I still feel forty-five."

She recalls how her counselors would run to the mail room after lunch, hoping to find letters from their soldier boyfriends, overseas in World War II, and how much she loved tennis, canoeing, and fishing.

"Those were some of the very best years of life," she says softly. "I'm really proud that I got my Big C badge for canoeing. I still have my canoe paddle, with my name painted on it. Oh, how

I loved fishing. We would bring back the fish and cook them at our campsite. It was heaven.

"Sometimes, if I can't sleep at night, I take three deep breaths and think of something wonderfully pleasant. So you know what I think about? I think about the lake. I think about going out in the rowboat and going fishing around the cove. I think about sitting in the boat with this little pole in my hand, and then I fall right asleep.

"I don't think of one of the many great European trips, to Italy or to France or to Prague. I think of camp."

Leni rose to the top rank of tennis players during her Agawak summers, a skill that grew stronger over the decades. She quit playing competitively in 2005, after coming in first place in doubles at her country club for fourteen years straight.

"Last year, I got on the court and started hitting with the pro," she says with a husky laugh. "I was still good. I feel like I'm a teenager when I'm on the court. I've never lost that camp spirit or energy. Once an Agawak girl, always an Agawak girl!"

The majority of post–Title IX camp girls today are already well-rounded athletes. They are on basketball, lacrosse, swim, soccer, and dance teams, often three at once. We went to camp to run around. They go to camp to wind down.

What I have noticed most since my return is that, unlike our era, some of the most popular activities now are creative and noncompetitive, such as candle making, jewelry making, ukulele, and, a favorite of mine, Hippie Living.

In this ode to the Age of Aquarius and flower power, the girls learn how to tie-dye T-shirts, make granola, and the art of henna tattooing. I often stop by Hippie Living and tell the girls stories about what it was like to be a genuine living hippie, who went to Grateful Dead concerts, drove around in a VW bus covered in daisy decals, and demonstrated against the Vietnam War.

I read them a poem I wrote for *Agalog* in 1967, at the height of the civil rights movement. The *Agalog* theme of the week was Peace and Equality:

Black and white, why the fight
Why aren't we all treated alike?

We're no different, don't you see?
We won't be at peace, until we're all free
Prejudiced people they're really so blind
When their reasons for ignorance, is all in their
  mind

I still assign Peace and Equality as an *Agalog* theme, and I am so impressed at how serious and wise the young writers are on this topic. They are, after all, a generation coming of age in a sharply divided United States. They recognize the importance of kindness and inclusion as the only paths toward peace.

They also are living in an increasingly diverse community at camp. Agawak has grown into a camper family of many different faiths and cultures that span Indian and Asian to Latina and Russian. One third of the staff is from other countries.

Here is a reflection from a 2015 *Agalog* article on how kindness to all people matters, written by Ruby Rosenheck, a camper from Los Angeles who was then ten:

Kindness. A powerful word with a powerful meaning.

Kindness is pretty much the only way to survive in our world. All of the great peace leaders are amazing because they are so kind.

Imagine, if all the people in the world were kind to each other. Then, there would be so much more peace.

We all have kindness in us—we just have to find it and use it.

Though much joy in camp life comes from perpetual busyness and action, I notice how content my writers like Ruby are, just to be still, rapt in their imagination. My friends from the old days are incredulous when I tell them that modern girls used to dashing off texts in truncated phrases while on the go are happy to be sitting for long stretches of time, and to handwrite for pages.

My friends also cannot believe there are no longer mandatory swimming and diving lessons, and that many girls choose to sit in Adirondack chairs on the beach and talk to each other, rather than even get wet.

I get it, though.

After six summers immersed in the new camp culture, I get that this generation of camp girls is straddling frenzied days of sports and academics back home. Summer camp provides a respite from their overscheduled lives, which can look like this: seven hours of school, followed by dance practice and a lacrosse game, a couple of hours of homework, and a couple of hours of Instagram and Snapchat.

A central attraction for these girls to return each summer is simply to be together in real time, off-line, to just chill. To be disconnected from all the beautiful people in beautiful places on social media that make them feel less beautiful and lonelier.

Wisconsin-bred Mary Fried took the lead of Camp Agawak in 1990, after receiving a master's degree in educational psychology and working as a social worker in the school system. From her front-row director's/owner's chair, she has witnessed the transformation of camp girls affected by the pressures of an evolving, fast-paced technological world.

The youngest of seven children and a long-distance runner, Mary, at fifty-three, has the spunk and lithe body of a twenty-five-year-old. She credits her indomitable effervescence and fitness to traversing the 250-acre camp several times a day. She always walks fast, trailed by the swish of her black ponytail.

Here is Mary's take on how giving children a place to just hang out is not only calming, but a "depression fighter."

MARY

I see far higher levels of anxiety in campers than I did when I started as a camp director thirty years ago. The structure and the support found at camp allows for our children to decompress from the stressors of their over-packed lives.

Camp is a natural anxiety fighter.

Giving children time to chill and spend time in nature is more important than ever before.

These children take ACT and SAT tests far earlier

now, and they take these tests three and four times. Even if they do better, they still feel like they're not good enough. To add to the academic pressure, they are stressed over the intense competition to make their school tennis teams, soccer teams, swim teams. Years ago, you walked on to a team.

Then there's the intense pressure of social media: How can they keep up with hundreds of screen friends that post only their happiest stories, their prettiest filtered poses surrounded by smiling friends? Girls with not so many smiling friends who may not feel so pretty are thinking, "Wow, everyone's life seems so much better than mine," which is depressing.

Social media is so often a false projection of one's life. Camp is real life.

At camp, the girls wear sweatpants and T-shirts, and their hair is tied up in messy ponytails. They aren't out-posting each other on Instagram; they are talking, not texting. They have the uninterrupted time to have deep and long conversations. It's in the quietest of moments in the cabin, whether during rest period or at bedtime, that the girls have the most significant conversations, they really open up to each other.

Something really important happens in the woods.

They begin to trust themselves more; they develop trust in each other. They share their deepest secrets about things they haven't shared with anybody. They talk about their worries, and it is healing, because they feel heard and that others care.

Along with the warmth of cabin life, nature in itself is very calming. Nature slows them down. Surrounded by a forest, they can really think, they can reflect. In their frenetic lives at home, they rarely have five minutes to stop, let alone the weeks we have at camp just to stop and breathe in the fresh air. Camp is truly an oasis, the place where girls can feel like they truly belong and are accepted for who they are.

Camp is love.

Though we jumped at the chance to flex our athleticism, we, too, craved the times when we just chilled together in leisurely activities. Though "chill" then didn't mean to hang out. The word was most commonly used when we were waking up, throwing off layers of blankets and the sweat clothes we slept in, and freezing as we pulled on navy pants, navy sweaters, and checkered wool lumber jackets. Many mornings temperatures would hover slightly above forty degrees.

As much as I loved hypersonic volleyball and tennis matches, some of my best memories are from when we were just lying on our beds and talking, during rest hour or in slow-rolling activities.

Those chill activities of yesteryear I still turn to today when I want to slow down.

I often bead bracelets like I learned to do in Arts & Crafts. I bake muffins in orange skins, like our guide, Al the Tripping Man, taught us to do on wilderness trips. Because of camp, I became conscious of the Zen of bed making, which now includes fashioning meticulous hospital corners and asking a family member to help me fold blankets into a three-part rectangle to go at the foot of our beds. We called it the "Agawak fold," but it is really the standard military fold.

This ritual always brings me back to Agawak, when we chattered with friends as we made those tight beds and swept the dust balls off the floor.

The "camp girl forever" spirit that Leni Landorf describes springs alive in countless other moments and places. The rush of reverie can stem from something as subtle as seeing a patch of reddish dirt sprinkled with pine needles in my Annapolis backyard. The response is instant as I am thrown back onto the reddish paths that lined the pine forests at Agawak. These paths of dirt always gave me the urge to go from a walk to a run, dodging the protruding roots, knowing I was headed for playtime with friends.

This exuberant charge also happens when I hear the slamming of my porch screen door. I am reminded of the many slams and screeching springs of screen doors we heard as we rushed in and out of our cabin to change for our activities. In the course of one day, we could change from slacks and sweaters, worn to breakfast, into boots and jeans for horseback riding; into swimsuits for waterskiing; back into long pants and long sleeves for hikes; back into our navy tank suits for instructional swimming; and into our blue shorts and white shirts for dinner.

I was talking to my cabinmate Karen Berk about the screech and slam of a screen door. We agree that the sound takes us back to the most carefree of days, when we were always bound toward the next best place.

"I felt like we were living like wild people in the woods, in this rustic cabin with a creaky door. It was so wonderful," says Karen. "Rushing in and out, the slam of the door, brings back the best memories of being engaged in nonstop activities. We always had something to do.

"When our children were young, we used to spend summers in a little cottage in the woods of Michigan," Karen adds. "It reminded me so much of camp. The people who lived behind us didn't like the noise of the screen door slamming in our house, kids going in and out all day. They put up a big sign that said 'Don't Slam the Door. It Bothers the Neighbors.' I knew immediately they never went to summer camp. I can never get enough of that sound."

Making my bed, the slam of a door, fallen pine needles, a ride in a kayak—the memories are jarringly real, so close to the surface are these soothing snapshots from deep in the past.

I keep the pink-and-turquoise suede bag holding my jumbo jacks and my rubber Super Ball next to my desk. When I play the game on the oak floor of my living room with my fifty-year-old friend Liz Klein Glass, the alumna of Camp Wohelo, we feel centered, transported, like little, joyful kids.

To the beat of the ball's bounce and the clink of the jacks, we share how things we see daily, the dirt trails and boats on the rivers that thread through our hometown, provide an undercurrent of serenity. These bastions of our childhood recharge us, at every age, to tackle our days with full-throttle energy to pursue a variety of people and adventures, like we did as kids.

I have summer camp to thank for my versatility, yet I am thinking of all the entrepreneurial non-camper people I admire who operate on many successful tracks. They may not have grown up in the deep woods of Wisconsin, yet I know they, too, are grounded somewhere in their youth, by loving friends and smart mentors who taught them the value of curiosity and stick-to-it-iveness.

Perhaps they, too, have a place they keep returning to that assembles all the disparate pieces of their lives into one unbroken timeline, a place that makes them feel ageless and whole.

Perhaps they, too, bloomed with abandon in

nature under an endless sky, surroundings that awakened their potential, their passions, the discovery of who they were meant to be—like we camp girls got to do.

Camp gave us elemental traits that I call the three Ps, passion, perseverance, and a positive attitude. These character builders developed because we felt supported and safe emotionally, knowing that if we were to fall, somebody would catch us.

One of my saddest camp memories is when we literally did pick someone up who fell to the ground: our friend JoAnn, who had just found out her older brother had been killed in a motorcycle accident. We cradled her, then got her to her feet, saying over and over, "We love you, JoAnn. We love you."

Agawak director Mary Fried says, "Camp is love." We hear the word "love" a lot at camp, and we mean it when we say it. Those words spoken there feel so different than the random "love yous" we casually spin out to end phone calls and emails.

We are in Margie Gordon's living room in suburban Chicago for a winter reunion of our camp-girl circle. I look around at the fourteen women, which include a midwife, an audiologist, a life coach, a graphic designer, a wealth manager, and a retail executive.

I see young children who worked hard every day to become the adults they are today, campers who lifted me up when I needed them and who I lifted up when they were in need. I see how we were transformed every day of every summer, making a homesick camper smile, forgiving someone who spewed hurtful words, saying "I'm sorry" to someone we hurt.

As campers, we received many trophies and badges for athletic excellence—awards we could feel with our hands. But the most substantive awards come from our acts of emotional excellence. These are notches on our psyches, soldered onto our character.

We also saw the lasting rewards of perseverance, a quality drilled into us as camp girls that has propelled many of us into long and fulfilling careers.

For me, it was writing *Agalog* articles that gave

me that sense of "Yes! This is who I was meant to be!" For Jan Levy, it was scribbling away, propped up on the bottom of our bunk bed before the morning bell, seeding her future as a lyricist and playwright.

As is the tradition at most summer camps, we wrote and sang songs for every occasion, after each meal, to chronicle our canoe trips, to honor our counselors, our captains, and our teams. We also had all-camp concerts, with each cabin making up original lyrics to replace those in popular songs.

Our go-to writer for all these occasions was Jan, who went from being our star songwriter to landing a production at Lincoln Center. Her trajectory began by spending a lot of time perusing the glass shelves of books in the director's cottage. There, she found *Poems That Live Forever*, a collection that included works by William Shakespeare, Elizabeth Barrett Browning, and Ralph Waldo Emerson. It was these melodic verses, she tells me, that released her own rhythm and forever changed her life.

At the age of thirty-five, in the role of what

Jan calls "an uninspired stay-at-home mom," she reignited her camp passion by enrolling in a course called Successful Lyric Writing at the New School in New York City. Then, after relocating to her hometown of Chicago, she started working on musicals.

Jan wrote the lyrics for the show *A Minister's Wife*, based on *Candida* by George Bernard Shaw, which played at the Chicago Writers Theatre in 2009. Two years later, *A Minister's Wife* moved to Lincoln Center's Newhouse Theater. She also wrote the lyrics for *Crazy Mary Lincoln* with composer Jay Schwandt; a reading of that show was featured at the Kennedy Center in Washington, DC, in 2015.

I asked Jan what comes to mind for her when she thinks back to the place where she found the poet-within:

JAN

The first word that comes up is "freedom." At camp, I felt like my creativity and energy could spread out as far as the eyes could see. I really liked my English classes in school, but there was always a curriculum. Camp was the first place I felt like I wasn't in a container, and I could let my spirit take me wherever it wanted to go.

The opportunity to start writing songs was something I immediately loved to do. Using the existing tunes from musicals and pop culture, I found I could easily find the words. I didn't feel like I had to do anything for anyone's approval, like in school. It was a freedom I hadn't felt since I was a kid on the playground. It was also a sense of accomplishment I hadn't experienced before. I got so much praise at camp for my songs, and that is an ego boost that goes a long way.

In college, I never took a creative writing course. I was too terrified about not doing it right, scared to be freely expressive outside the camp environment. Then in my thirties with two young sons, I was a frustrated stay-at-home mom, desperate to figure out what to do.

I read a biography of Carl Jung, and when he was trying to figure out the right journey for his life, he reflected on what he loved to play as a child. So I started thinking about what I loved, and it was writing songs. In the Successful Lyric Writing class, our assignment was to write three songs. After the teacher reviewed mine, she said: "You're a pro!"—and I burst into tears and hugged her. That led to writing more musicals and to Lincoln Center! The spark for all of this came from a little camp library, some fifty years ago.

Camp unearthed the creative part of me. At camp, I found my voice.

I am thinking of one of the most beautiful camp songs that Jan wrote in 1970, titled "Blue Lake Waters," sung to the tune of the Bee Gees' "Turn Around, Look at Me." We sing this song at our reunions, and it makes us cry, as we are flooded with visions of our younger selves singing this while setting birch-bark wish boats out to sail the last night of camp.

After a round of "Blue Lake Waters," we cannot speak, lost in verses like this:

Blue Lake's waters glisten before us,
Trees of pine guard our shores,
Wooden cabins cling to the hillside,
Light blue sky, so serene.

In our camp life, we will establish
All our hopes, all our dreams

I am humming "Blue Lake Waters" as I sort out clothes to pack for the summer of June 2019, imagining the glisten of the lake, my oasis. Just from the act of packing, I already sense a diffusing of stress, a shift from dressing up to dressing down. I feel the freedom that Jan describes, that soon my spirit will no longer be contained.

The pile of clothes includes the checkered flannel shirt I have had since the summer of 1963, a shirt saturated in the scent of pine and fire. I bury my face in the fabric and I think of my departed mother who bought me that shirt at Sears, mine in blue and white, and one for my sister, in red and white.

My mom would not let us wear flannel shirts or casual camp clothes to school, though I wanted to, to cling to summer. "You would luke like a veggabond!" she would say, in her thick accent.

I would wear that shirt on the bus to camp, the mode of transportation that replaced trains in 1965, and I wear it at camp today. The flannel is still soft and warm, though fraying at the elbows. It is functional in air-conditioned buses and on cool campfire nights.

In that shirt and in all my sloppy camp attire, I never felt like a vagabond, a wanderer without a home. I was always wandering back to the same place, a home of roots and wings and certainty.

As a child, I returned from camp brown and muscled, holding my lanyards and trophies and so much love. I would tell my parents, "I can do anything."

Camp made me feel that way at eight, and I feel that way now as I hike the Agawak hills and keep up with young girls. The russet-red dirt on the trails that circle my camp and my house, where I moved as a newlywed and raised four sons, arc the circle of my life.

Chapter Five
Nature

"In the simple perfection of nature, I am thrust into a restoration of self, an excavation of mental debris, a knowing: This is who I was meant to be all along."

The start of Robert Frost's poem "Stopping by Woods on a Snowy Evening," though describing the cold, reminds me of the woods of summer, and the peace of nature that gives us peace within:

Whose woods these are I think I know

Whose woods are these? These woods are mine. I claimed them as a girl, and I own them as a woman. Walking up camp hills and over roots I know the shape and location of instinctively, I am anchored in the landscape I memorized as a child.

The woods make us stop and be grateful. Unconsciously, we practice mindfulness, the cultural "it word," although it is the ancient core of Hinduism and Buddhism.

Nature shakes us into a primal aliveness.

Nature helps us learn, and can inspire future environmentalists, we are reminded by prominent child development educator Peg Smith, formerly the CEO of the American Camp Association.

"I've worked with youth at state and federal levels, in schools, Head Start, disability programs, teen development programs, and childcare," says Peg. "And when I walk into a camp community, hands down, this is the best learning landscape I've seen for young children and young adults.

"Learning outdoors, in nature, children become aware that more needs to be done to preserve our environment. The environment needs to be *experienced* to be appreciated. Kids need to catch tadpoles in the creek, wander among the trees, and feel the sun on their faces to understand the importance of those things. The leaders of tomorrow will suffer a lack of vision if they have never experienced the magic of seeing the stars in the dark of night."

This Chicago-reared girl has made a permanent home in a rural Maryland habitat where stars shine brightly because of camp, with an ex-camper spouse, with whom we raised camper kids.

My husband—a.k.a. Wood Chuck—is an architect and woodworker from a rural Maryland town. I married him for five reasons: He is a very nice guy. He is reliable. He is really good-looking. He loved his own summer camp, where he worked washing dishes and driving the ski boat. Lastly, he prefers to live next to trees and not buildings.

We met in Washington, DC, and within the first four years of marriage, after our twins were born, we had four sons under the age of three. Knowing this litter would need open spaces to run, we moved to an expanse of land on a hill, on a river, nestled in arborvitae hedges and pines.

In our nearly three decades here, we wake up to foxes and groundhogs and deer, and turtles, the signature animal of our state. Seasoned by their own summers at Raquette Lake, our boys still build fires and sleep outdoors, and, like their parents, claim the woods as their choice refuge.

Our home and our land smell like camp.

Chuck expanded the small existing house and turned it into a large cedar shingled cabin. Several months a year, we eat at a picnic table on a screened porch overlooking the river. There, we have had hundreds of family meals of Maryland's signature blue crabs, corn, and tomatoes. The whirl of our work lives is soothed by the view of the water, dotted with paddleboarders and tilting sailboats.

Food tastes better and lasts longer in nature.

Noticing the sweetness of every kernel of corn and every lump of crab, I am reminded of how often I rush through a meal to get to a meeting, surprised when my plate is empty with no recollection of what I ate.

I have sat for hours at the weathered and stained picnic table on the porch. And not a meal goes by that I am not tossed back onto Agawak's picnic tables and shingled cabins, and into a seesaw of emotions, and layers of memories.

During those camper meals with raucous friends, food was jettisoned from our mouths through gapes of laughter. Revved up on sports and each other, we surged with adrenaline until we collapsed into sleep.

As an adult, I have grown to appreciate the power of stopping, cushioned by trees, subdued by an endless sky.

On the frenzied Severn River kayak excursion, I paddled with urgency, submerged in a fantasy trance of a war-canoe race from long ago. When I am kayaking on Blue Lake as a staff member, I am consciously lily-dipping, lazily, with no screaming critics or commands rousing my mind.

As a young camp girl embroiled in the heat of outdoor competition, I was more focused on winning games than the calm of nature. As a grown-up camp girl who has lived more of life than she has left to live, I have come to believe that the most important game to master is the art of slow-ing down, and to find purpose and fulfillment at every stage.

So far, nature is making that dream come true.

In the latest rendition of myself at Agawak, I like to rise before the 8 a.m. bell to kayak on a lake that is like glass. I stop paddling as I pull up to a loon and her baby, quiet for now, though later I will hear the mother's haunting call. The sound of the loon reverberates at the level of soul.

There is a stillness that is pure and empty and cleansing on Blue Lake, drowning the incessant chatter of the mind that depletes my ability to be present in the present. A mug of hot coffee in my hand, the paddle straddled across the bow, I am clearheaded and aware and thankful.

What else could I want?

In the simple perfection of nature, I am thrust into a restoration of self, an excavation of mental debris, a knowing: This is who I was meant to be all along.

My kayak begins to sway gently, caused by rip-ples from a small fishing boat passing by. The driver is holding a coffee cup and a fishing pole, and he smiles. We do not talk, but I know what he knows and he knows what I know—that on this glorious morning in balmy July, we are two of the luckiest people alive.

I reach the shore and pull up my boat on the beach. Walking to my cabin, the only sounds I hear are my flip-flops on the dirt path and a couple of chipmunks scurrying in front of me. And then comes the exclamation mark on this stretch of nothingness: the call of the loon in the distance, a call that will keep luring me back.

Counselors, then and now, would forbid a lone kayak ride by a camper at dawn. Today, this lake is mine. This forest has been mine since I first entered it.

The woods are lovely, dark and deep,
But I have promises to keep,
And miles to go before I sleep.

As I read these lines in the last stanza of Robert Frost's poem, I do not have miles to go before I sleep. I am home the moment I see the Agawak sign at the entrance of camp, crafted out of split logs.

Frost's character is compelled to keep walking to somewhere else. My promise to myself is to stop, in the lovely forests of Maryland and Wisconsin. And though the woods are dark and deep, and sometimes cold, they will forever feel warm and comforting.

I know it is a sacred privilege to have been christened by nature at an early age, and to have lived much of my six decades in the natural world. I will work for the rest of my days to support ongoing efforts to give any child who wants to go to summer camp that opportunity.

I spoke with Jane Sanborn about how fortunate I feel to have spent most of my life in the woods and on water. Jane knows these sentiments so well, having been involved in the camping industry for fifty-two of her seventy years. She is the director of development for Sanborn Western Camps in Colorado, which operates Big Spring Ranch for Boys and High Trails Ranch for Girls.

"Whether it is hiking a trail or climbing a mountain or sailing a river, there is that sense of wonder and awe in the natural world," says Jane, who began her career in camping as a counselor at High

Trails. "It is one of those intangibles that happens all the time at camp. At camp, there is magic at every turn."

My forays into the woods are indeed magical, in northern Wisconsin and on the Baltimore & Annapolis Trail, which is often framed by wild-flowers in hues plucked from a crayon box. Walking has been my lifetime sport.

From girlhood to motherhood to empty-nesting with my husband in a large house, I have walked through many seasons and many moods, through tunnels of darkness, into the light. I walked through the death of my parents, and the transition of my children from infants to college graduates, and the celebration of my firstborn's thirtieth birthday.

I walked through unspeakable grief when five of my colleagues were slaughtered by a shooter in the newsroom of the *Annapolis Capital Gazette* where I am a Sunday columnist. I walk through my angst about the havoc in our world. I walk to stay fit and elongate my life span, so I can be here to feel the velvety cheeks of babies born to my sons whose faces are bristly with stubble.

I walk to listen to my heart in silence, where its truth can be heard.

I walk to sing camp songs with my phone partner Liz Weinstein.

My early evening walks end with me in my kitchen, sipping J. Lohr cabernet and looking at the river through pine trees. My mind stretches quickly to the shores of Blue Lake and the Wisconsin woods. In a blink, I am here, then I am there. Then as the wine warms me, I think of my mother's voice and the talks about little and big things we used to share at the kitchen table, from preferred lipstick shades to our hard comeback from the sudden death of her husband and my father.

Memories of our mother-daughter exchanges that ranged from the superficial to the unthinkable can be haunting.

We make idle conversations with our parents, thinking there will always be another time to excavate all the deeper subjects, about their own childhoods, about their roads not taken. My mom and I often spoke about my dad's death. We did not speak often enough about my mom's life.

Then she was gone.

I have profiled hundreds of people during a lengthy journalism career, from cabdrivers to movie stars, extracting the most minute of details of their histories. There are so many, too many, questions I never asked my mother.

How did she manage to dodge Nazis and survive during fifteen years of Europe's German occupation? I know she took on a false Christian-sounding identity that erased her last name of Steinberg, a Jewish giveaway.

What else did she have to do?

Remorse over the should haves and could haves brings on a knot in the gut that eventually morphs into a smile, as some vivid scenes that I know *did* happen flash into my mind's eye.

I see my mother running to my sister and me, with open arms and screaming our names, when she and my father arrived at camp for Parents' Weekend. She was always the first to race to her children, and she definitely was the loudest.

Not knowing all the paths in our parents' past is not as important as knowing how much we were loved. In the work that I do writing books about relationships, I have found that this is what triggers the most sadness and regret: A mom or dad dies, and the son or daughter never heard "I love you," or never closed an old wound, remaining in a stubborn standoff from an old fight. Then they realize, too late, you cannot say "I'm sorry" at a funeral.

I believe my mother and father loved me even more when I got back from camp; I was more sure-footed, more helpful, more of everything.

On my walks in the woods, I am infused with nostalgia as my mind rewinds to the cherished places of a lifetime ago. I may become my six-year-old self, playing mancala on a picnic bench at Travelaire Day Camp. I can almost hear the ping of the stones when they are dropped into the little cups of the game's wooden board.

I may become my forty-year-old self, a mother of two babies and two toddlers, pulling up their high chairs to the picnic bench on our porch, fastening on plastic Big Bird bibs, then spooning smashed peas into tiny pink mouths.

Those mouths always reminded me of the tiny mouths of the birds that peck sunflower seeds at our feeder.

Yesterday, I walked through a foggy morning in Annapolis that felt like I was going to flag raising at Agawak, where many mornings are fogged by mist. It is surreal, yet so very real, how so many thoughts, and all roads, lead back to picnic tables and back to camp.

The walks I take on the Baltimore & Annapolis Trail would be only a warm-up for Margie Gordon, a camper of my era who has also worked on the Agawak staff. Margie remains an All-Around Camper, the coveted title she won in 1968, given to the most versatile athlete and all-around good person. Her chestnut-brown shoulder-length blunt cut has only recently sprouted a few gray hairs, and her calves are bands of muscle.

Margie was always the most adept of us in camp-craft skills. She was the one who could wield a heavy axe and use the dull side to hammer in stakes for our tents, then start a one-match fire in the rain. She tells me that she considers Agawak's wilderness trip guide, Al Gabrilska—we called him

Papa Al—"one of the most inspirational people in my life."

I can visualize Al now, paddling in the stern of his canoe, with Lady, his black Labrador retriever, sitting upright in the bow. Al was six foot four and built like Paul Bunyan. Five-foot-four Margie seems to have channeled his talents and spirit.

During our alumni reunions, Margie leads the hikes and, at sunset, builds the fire in the pit, after chopping some large logs into kindling. At a recent gathering, the fire began to hiss from a light rain. Margie grabbed a black plastic tarp, spiked it to the ground, and roped it like a tent to a tree, to protect the flames.

We were making s'mores and realized we had the chocolate bars and graham crackers but had forgotten the marshmallows. "I'll go get them," said Margie, taking off at a lope to the other side of camp, where the kitchen was located, and returning in a few minutes with two bags of marshmallows. Her face was gleaming with sweat.

Our camp director, Mary, was so wowed by the irrepressible Margie that she tapped the all-around camper to join a group of counselors that lead overnight trips, teaching naturalist and survival skills to this generation of girls. They come away knowing fire building, outdoor cooking, how to identify constellations and plants, how to poop in the woods, how to leave no trace of garbage behind, how to honor nature.

Margie was a first-year camper in 1964, placed in Cabin 6 with my sister, Frances. I remember that Margie, a child of suburban Chicago just out of fifth grade, was immediately fearless in nature.

We had a bat in the lodge that would swoop down from the stage while we watched plays and movies at night. Most girls would shriek and cover their heads. Not Margie. A fan of all animals, she would stand up and watch in awe this creature we called Swinger, named for his routine swings through the wooden rafters.

Aside from Swinger fright, how all of us loved those movie nights, viewing *new* films like *Swiss Family Robinson*, *Mary Poppins*, and *The Sound of Music*. Counselors set up a stand with an assortment of candies, like those offered at real movie theaters, and each girl could select one item before the show began. I veered toward Milk Duds and Chuckles, favoring the black licorice ones.

Along with her nonchalance at flying mammals, Margie endured the elements better than the rest of us. In the coldest of weather, as we layered up in down, she would wear a light parka.

Though I am a fast walker, I still cannot keep up with Margie on hikes. She has always been charging ahead, in all aspects of her outdoorsmanship.

The trip she considers her best vacation was four weeks of backpacking with her then-husband and their sons above the Arctic Circle in Alaska, sleeping in a cabin with no electricity and no running water. There were no other people around for twenty miles, in any direction.

For her thirtieth birthday, Margie led her family, including her mother and grandmother, on a camping excursion into remote areas of Wisconsin. At the age of fifty, she was certified as a yoga instructor.

Like me, this woodswoman says she was significantly shaped by her exposure to nature at summer camp. When she speaks about her love of camping, she has to stop often as she chokes up with emotion.

We camp girls laugh and cry a lot.

MARGIE

I have traveled the entire world, and still one of the most beautiful places to me is that little cove on Blue Lake. I remember feeling this overwhelming sense of wonder, and that nature was a refuge. Since then, nature has become a lifelong refuge, where I seek solace and peace.

That same sense of wonder and consummate respect for nature is what I try to give each girl today on camping trips. We lie on our backs, stargazing and noticing how the outline of the trees is like a picture frame for the campsite.

Though long gone, Papa Al remains my steadfast guide, as the leader who taught us how to honor nature, to leave only footprints and take away only memories. He taught us how to wash plates with sand on the shores of our campsites. He taught us how to pack only the essentials in a very small bag.

He would say, "If you can't carry it, don't bring it."

To this day, I hear his voice as he showed us the art of fire building: how to collect kindling, tinder, and build a tepee in the middle with a log cabin around it. His fires took one match, and mine do, too.

I would get up very early, and he showed me how to build a no-match fire for breakfast by fanning some little ember from the fire the night before.

We never felt afraid as we huddled somewhere safe in our canoes, as storms came raging across the lake. We watched spectacular shows ablaze with lightning, in awe of the power of nature. One time, we had to lie across the gunnels of our canoes so the thrashing wind wouldn't blow us away.

Those lessons, that awe of nature, became part of my DNA, and I passed it along. By the time they were six months old, each of our three sons had been camping, sleeping under the stars in portable cribs.

Those boys have turned my love of nature into an art form. One son summited Mount McKinley at the age of seventeen. They all backcountry ski, blazing their own trails. All three have done triathlons.

When I think about what gives me the most pride in raising our children, now ages thirty-two to forty-two, what comes up is that they have the same reverence for

Mother Nature as their mom. No matter what happens in the world, they know what I know, that we can always find peace in the mountains, on a lake, in the woods.

While living in the wild does spark a reverence for nature and campfires, lots more is sparked, too. As we turned into teens and our hormones amped up, many of us camp girls found that nature unleashed our yearning for romance.

The summer between eighth grade and freshman year, a friend and I had big crushes on two of the stable hands. We would sneak out at 5:30 a.m. to shovel manure, to help brush the horses, and to just be in the barn with Joe and Sam, both sixteen. They were craggy, rough-talking farm boys, way grittier and groovier than the slick city boys back home.

Smelly and swooning, we would then race back to our cabin by 7 a.m., and slip back into our pajamas. When the morning bell rang shortly after, we would yawn, stretch our arms, and pretend to be waking up with the rest of the group.

These woods of mine, and ours, glorified by Robert Frost, also aroused lots of other sneaky gallivants during socials with the boys' camps.

For these much-anticipated evenings, we could ditch our blue-and-white uniforms and turn up the glamour.

In the style of the seventies, in the waning stages of the mod movement, out came the halters and clingy tank tops, the short shorts and paisley bell-bottoms. Out came the Covergirl blush, Yardley Slicker lip glosses, the turquoise and lavender eye shadows.

We would dance with the boys and with each other: to songs playing on a record player in the darkened lodge, doing the Swim to the Beach Boys' "Wouldn't It Be Nice" and slow-dancing to the Association's "Cherish."

Inevitably, one of us "fell in love" and retreated into the woods for a make-out session. If you got caught missing and kissing during a social, you got benched from activities for a day. We covered for each other when a counselor would ask about a girl she could not find, explaining: "She went to the bathroom."

One night during a social with Camp Kawaga, our counselor Tammy was asking around, "Has anyone seen Rebecca?"

Rebecca had been dancing with a very handsome, very tall boy, and we all saw them head for the door. We used the bathroom line, but then in the morning, at the sink, we saw a mark on her neck the color and size of a plum—my first hickey sighting.

In horror and haste before the counselors woke up, we grabbed a tube of flesh-tinted Clearasil and caked it over the evidence. Rebecca sat out of swimming for two days, feigning to waterfront director Beaver that it was "that time of the month" and she had bad cramps.

My own first open-mouth kiss happened at a camp social the summer of the hickey. There is nothing like romance under the stars, encased by trees.

Long before I married a guy who loves the woods, I left an outdoorsy guy I thought could be The One. At a winter rendezvous, I swiftly found out that summer-camp love could fizzle once transferred from under the stars to under fluorescent lights.

I was eighteen and he was twenty-four, the waterskiing instructor at a boys' camp close by. This was a time when the drinking age was eighteen, and staff from all the surrounding camps would mingle at local bars, where we would drink foaming mugs of Wisconsin brews, like Miller, Schlitz, and Pabst.

My summer boyfriend was always in worn jeans and hiking boots crusted with mud. He played guitar and sang like Bob Dylan, eyes closed, whiny, the sexiest man alive.

I fell in love, well, lust, with this guy on my first night out as a counselor during the summer of 1973, and we dated through the camp season. Dates meant leaving the bar together and heading for the woods. In a letter home, I wrote vaguely of my summer love:

Dear Mom & Dad, I met the man of my dreams this summer. Ha! Don't worry. He is Jewish!

He was a Christian Scientist. That, too, added to his appeal, as a foreigner to my culture, new territory to explore. Not only could he barefoot-ski, but he spoke of how he could heal himself without drugs or medical intervention.

This came from the teachings of the founder of Christian Science, Mary Baker Eddy, who claimed in her 1875 book *Science and Health* that "sickness is an illusion that can be corrected by prayer alone."

The summer of '73 was incredibly hot: the weather, my ardor, and in so many other naughty and wondrous ways.

I returned to college in California, but Wisconsin nights with Mr. Hubba-Hubba stuck with me, in my heart and other places. We exchanged sexy letters that fall semester of my junior year, making vague plans to see each other soon. I was both scared and ecstatic when his December letter included a plane ticket for me to arrive on a Friday and leave on a Monday morning to his hometown in Nebraska. (This was way before e-tickets.)

I called him collect that night from the pay phone in the Palo Alto restaurant where I was a waitress and said exuberantly, "I'll be there." And he said, "I'll be there, too"—waiting for me at the gate.

Our reunion lasted twenty minutes. My tanned and rugged paramour from the backwoods looked like Darrin from the TV show *Bewitched*: bland and white and way too clean. Gone were the jeans and work boots, the coarse machismo. He was wearing a navy blazer and khaki trousers that rode two inches above shiny loafers that held shiny pennies.

His floppy sun-streaked hair of July was now shorn and dark brown, leaving me thinking he had been spraying Sun-In that summer of sun-kissed love. Beyond superficial appearances, without camp in common, we stood awkwardly in silence after he asked, "How was the flight?"

As he went in for an embrace, there was a wrench in my heart that was not of yearning, but of "Damn, what have I done?" Away from the pine forest, he was definitely not my type. I had carried on board a small leather bag, had not checked luggage, and realized quickly what I had to do. I had to bolt.

I conjured up some tears and spouted a blur of words I cannot recall precisely but that went something like this: "This feels weird...We are a camp thing…Maybe I will see you next summer." He said he was not returning. I kissed him on the cheek, said I would send him a check for my plane fare, and ran to the ticket counter to secure the first flight back to San Francisco, without looking back.

I am not proud of the hurt I know this must have caused him—he later described his shock in a letter—watching me literally run away. I am proud that I did not do something I did not want to do, though I should have written him back.

It was an enduring lesson in trusting my gut, and it clarified the type of partner that I am most suited for: earthy year-round. Chuck is rugged, inside and out.

Many of my Agawak friends also married nature-loving partners who had attended summer camp. As we kept in touch during our college years, we would share how our instincts about whether a relationship had a chance to survive usually came back to: "Are they camp people?"

During the colder seasons, I have watched the film *Indian Summer* with my children more than a dozen times, to be back with camp people, to revive our camp selves. The 1993 film portrays the return of a group of eight ex-campers, now in their late twenties, to Camp Tamakwa, summoned by the camp's owner/director Lou Handler, a.k.a. Uncle Lou played by Alan Arkin.

Written and directed by Mike Binder, who attended Tamakwa for ten summers, *Indian Summer* is filmed at the actual camp, which is still in operation, in heavily wooded Algonquin Park outside of Toronto, on South Tea Lake.

As the story unfolds, these boys and girls who once paired off on teams and in romances become hot and amorous again, inflamed by surroundings that toss them back in time. Dealing with unresolved affections results in new romantic pairings and some heartbreak.

I could watch this movie a hundred more times. When the Tamakwa alumni are canoeing and swimming, competing in relays and reigniting first loves, this is my camp, it is every camper's camp. We all experience a re-awakening of those emotions that are piqued to high intensity by images of see-through lakes, of stolen kisses while backed up to trees, of being hurled into some of the most thrilling moments of our lives.

Torrid summer love can combust into more than a fleeting romance. Some of those camp girls and camp boys who became infatuated with each other in the woods and on the waterfront are now couples in lifelong partnerships, like Heidi and Bruce Katz, who met at nineteen, at Surprise Lake Camp and have been married for forty years.

Laurie Pearson met Chris Browne the summer of 2000 at Otto's, still a popular Minocqua, Wisconsin, beer garden, when they were both working as wilderness trip leaders at camps. She was on staff at Clearwater Camp for Girls; he worked at Camp Timberlane for Boys. After a year of dating long-distance, as he was based in Toronto and she was in Chicago, Chris surprised Laurie the following summer and proposed to her one early evening at her flag-lowering ceremony.

Chris had paddled solo in his canoe to Clearwater, then stood in front of Laurie's entire camp to ask his girlfriend to be his wife.

"I don't remember exactly what he said, only that it included showing me a canoe paddle that he carved by hand and engraved with 'Will you marry me?'" says Laurie. "The ring, a family heirloom, was taped to the blade of the paddle with duct tape. We got married on that very spot a year later, and continue to visit Clearwater with our three children, ages fifteen, twelve, and ten. And we named our black Labrador 'Otto.'"

Denise Morris, fifty, began her eight years as a camper and counselor at Agawak in the mid-1970s. And on these cherished grounds, in the setting of nature, she met her future husband Dean Salit, an alumnus of Timberlane who was then the Agawak wilderness guide.

"I was twenty when we met," says Denise. "It was late at night, and this guy walked into my cabin to tell me one of the rowboats was unhooked and floating in the middle of the lake. Here I was, one of the leaders of camp, and I said: 'Okay, I better figure this out.'

"He said, 'Don't worry. I'll take care of it.' Then he hopped into a canoe and rescued the rowboat. I was drawn to his take-charge attitude. From his own camping experience, Dean grew up to be this man who knows everything about surviving in the woods and fishing and crossing lakes and cooking over a fire. I was not that athletic or much for canoe trips, though we are both camp people. We understand each other on a very deep level. When we met, we were just friends for a while. But things move very quickly at camp."

Denise's last summer as a young staff member was thirty years ago. She and Dean went on to raise two sons and a daughter, also an Agawak girl. In the summer of 2019, Denise came back to fill the position of activity director. We are reunited as camp sisters who left Agawak decades ago, like children who leave home searching for identity in a smattering of other cities, only to return to plant roots in their hometowns.

Minocqua, Wisconsin, is not our real place of birth, but in so many ways it's our place of rebirth.

Chapter Six

Responsibility

"With no Mommy or Daddy around, we quickly learned the necessity of taking care of each other."

In June of 1963, after a jerky overnight train ride, too much red licorice, and not enough sleep, five of us very young girls were led to Cabin 3 by our counselors Tina and Ellen.

They were wearing starched white shirts, navy Bermuda shorts, and smiles that seemed a little too big as they expressed some cheery words of welcome. The sentence I remember most was this declaration, given with stony expressions: "You will become responsible young ladies this summer."

I could spell "responsible" but did not really know the meaning of the word, only that my third-grade teacher, Miss Kuntz, used it often to reprimand the class clown, Thomas. She would tell him that "responsible" was something he was not.

My understanding of the word changed quickly as Tina showed us a large sheet of cardboard on the back of the door. On it were stick figures of girls with our names in capital letters across the chests. Below the drawings, there was a list of five chores that we would be responsible for completing each day, and alternating each week.

That first week, I was assigned to sweeping.

Tina handed me a broom and told me to make sure I crawled on the floor and got all the dust balls out from under the beds. She then handed me a Folgers coffee can filled with what looked like nuggets of red rubber and smelled like gasoline.

She explained that this was "compound," and that I should sprinkle it around, to best clump together the dirt. As camp progressed, sweeping the cabin would dredge up other debris, like wrappers from the candy that our parents sent and our counselors only doled out at rest hour as we read our Archie comic books.

We made our beds at home, but my mom did the sweeping. She would whisk through the kitchen, slightly bent over, leaving a few stray bristles of straw from the broom behind. Learning this task, which I had only seen adults do, made me feel like what my father insisted I was: "a big, strong girl." This when I had cowered about leaving home that first summer.

Since that first time maneuvering a broom over a rough wooden floor, I have loved to sweep. I find the job meditative and satisfying, in mindful movement, and the goal is always accomplished. Unlike many desired goals in which efforts do not guarantee results, with a broom and a dustpan and hitting every corner, floors always end up spotless.

I felt even bigger and stronger as I mastered other cabin tasks—cleaning the toilet and sink, straightening the bathing suits and towels on the clothesline, and raking the entrance to the cabin, making sure I got rid of all the crusty leaves and left perfect rows of parallel lines in the dirt. Oh, how I adored the rich color of camp dirt, the rusty shade of a barn, and it seemed so clean, not like the dirty dirt of the city.

Taking responsibility for the care of our cabins streamed into deeper arteries of our lives well beyond housekeeping. With no Mommy or Daddy around, we quickly learned the necessity of taking care of each other. One of Peggy Gilbert's earliest Agawak memories was as an eight-year-old in 1964. A bunkmate was sobbing after dropping a suitcase on her foot. She was not hurt but was still yelping "I want to go home to my parents!"—who were a thousand miles away in Oklahoma.

The girls of Cabin 1 formed a group hug around her. "We held her until she stopped crying," says Peggy. "It was instinctive. In our small cabin, we immediately felt like a bedroom of sisters."

Margie Gordon recalls that those camp sisters continued to be a circle of support and love throughout her most brutal of grown-up hardships. Margie was in her early twenties when her older brother, Bruce, died of a brain tumor. Then, when she was in her early sixties, Margie's thirty-year marriage ended in divorce.

"My camp friends were always the safety net, a grounding force," Margie says softly. "Time and time again, they have reminded me of who I am, resilient and strong. Camp sisters show us, in the toughest of times, that we will never be alone."

All of us, every day of every summer, witnessed caregiving exemplified from the very top, by camp director Oscar Siegel. His wife, Natalie, had severe multiple sclerosis, which had put her in a wheelchair and with blurred speech, though her mental functioning was sharp. Their daughter, Renee, an only child, was born with cystic fibrosis.

We watched Oscar wheel Natalie up and down hills at camp, and lift her out of her chair and up steps and onto chairs in the dining room. We watched Oscar disappear several times a day into his cottage to conduct breathing treatments for Renee, to loosen the mucus in her lungs, which thickens with her disease. We watched selfless, painstaking acts of love and caregiving.

We suffered with Oscar as we watched Natalie and Renee grow weaker every summer—this as they watched campers grow more robust. Oscar was only sixty when he died of heart failure shortly after Renee passed away in her early thirties.

We camp girls believe he died of a broken heart after burying his daughter. Natalie died in 2010, outliving her husband by twenty years.

We learned a lot from this family.

Feeling responsible for each other's well-being as children often fans out into developing a penchant for leadership and service. This trio of traits that we are groomed to have at camp often become the drivers of choices we make in adulthood, personally and professionally.

Most of my Agawak friends, along with the dozens of lifers I know representing other camps, have gravitated toward careers centered on empowering others. Many are teachers and professors, like me; others have become healers or administrators in medical fields, or in nonprofit work focused on mental health. They are serving in leadership positions, in law, in business, in their communities, and in their charity work.

They may not have risen to *People* magazine fame, like this formidable group of ex–camp girls: Facebook COO Sheryl Sandberg, actor/comedian Whoopi Goldberg, and Supreme Court justice Ruth Bader Ginsburg. But any camper who spends several weeks in the woods and sticks with it, summer after summer, comes to exhibit tenacity, diligence, and responsibility.

We were handed dustpans and brooms as small children, and taught to nab every candy wrapper and ball of dust. We learned to spring back from a loss in team competition and to try harder to crush it the next time around. We slept in tents and heard animals cry in the night—and did not cry ourselves.

We were taught by role models like Oscar, and by each other, to brave adversity and not run from it. It helps that we gained inner strength in numbers and realized, as Margie Gordon puts it: "We are never alone."

I am remembering the words of Terry Worth, who likened herself to the supporting cast member Rhoda compared to some of her Agawak friends, whom she thought of as stars like Mary

Tyler Moore. Being the loyal sidekick played out in Terry's adult life in the most honorable way, though, as she took on a huge responsibility, to serve and to lead.

The girls in our oldest cabins are assigned "little sisters," new campers to mentor throughout the summer. Terry's was Lisa Citow Newman, with whom she stayed connected long after our camper years. At the age of forty-nine, Lisa died of ovarian cancer, in the fall of 2010. She left behind her husband of eighteen years and two young daughters.

During Lisa's illness, Terry had been working as an assistant for Lisa's brother, neurosurgeon Jonathan Citow. His wife, Karen, asked Terry to step in and help the grieving family.

Terry then became Terry Poppins:

TERRY

My life changed forever because of the Agawak connection.

Karen called and said that Lisa's biggest concern before she passed away was "Who's going to take care of my girls?" I knew the family well, as I worked for

Karen's husband and my daughter had been Lisa's regular babysitter.

And so I became Terry Poppins.

I could never replace Lisa, but I helped to raise those girls from fourth grade until they were each in their freshman year in high school. I got them off to school in the morning, ate dinner with them, did homework with them, then put them to bed. I did Friday night Shabbat with them and helped run a kosher house.

I brought the Agawak spirit into their home, singing camp songs and giving those kids as much unconditional love as I gave my own three kids, who were out of college and grown. I gave those girls the safe and structured environment that Agawak gave me.

At camp, we learned to roll up our sleeves and go to work when we were needed. We learned to love our friends like sisters. We learned to work together and contribute to the greater good of our team. This was Team Citow, and this time I was the captain. I was Mary, not Rhoda.

Lisa fought like an Agawak girl. She had ovarian cancer for fourteen years before she finally lost the battle.

Terry also points to her tenure as a longtime

counselor as important conditioning in her ability to become a responsible leader whose goal is to help others live better. Bobby Fisher, co-owner of Kawaga, our brother camp for boys, feels so intensely about the value of the counselor experience that when his former campers hesitate to return as staff because they want to gain "real-world experience" in an internship, he gives them this advice:

"I tell them being a camp counselor is better than an internship. As an intern, the extent to which you get to utilize real-life skills is limited. As a camp counselor, you are taking on a huge responsibility at a young age, and applying those life skills to help children become better human beings. As an intern, you are a follower; as a counselor, you emerge as a leader."

Leadership and responsibility clearly come to mind when I think of former counselors I admire most. Jill Klein, the dean of the School of Professional and Extended Studies at American University, is a fourteen-year veteran of sleep-away camps, including those spent in the Adirondack Mountains at Camp Red Wing, and summers at Quanset Camp and Camp Avalon on Cape Cod.

Jill Klein stands barely five feet tall, though she is known on the campus where I work as a professor as a larger-than-life dynamo, a person with big ideas who puts her visions into action.

As dean of the School of Professional and Extended Studies, Jill oversees programs and faculty that serve some one thousand students. She attributes her work ethic, which has led to leadership positions on Wall Street and in academia, as a "natural progression" from her responsibilities at camps.

"You learn quickly how to solve people problems as a camp counselor," says Jill. "At Avalon, I managed a staff of twenty other counselors and made sure a hundred twenty campers sailed every day. With that management training at the age of twenty-one, from there I have felt that I can lead any group, in any profession."

I am reminded again of how our counselors told us eight- and nine-year-olds starting our first summer at camp that we were about to become "responsible young ladies." As I listen to Jill's story and those from my extensive circle of ex-camper friends, I realize that this label does seem to embody what happens as we apply camp lessons and go forward as adults, driven to empower others.

In her four-year term as the first female president of the village of Winnetka in suburban Chicago, Louise Holland helped navigate solutions for housing, economic, and diversity challenges for a population of eighteen thousand.

Laurie Holleb helps substance abusers and their families as a certified alcohol and drug counselor.

Liz Weinstein is the founder of the Agawak Alumnae Foundation, which helps girls from underserved backgrounds by providing scholarships to summer camp.

As a partner in a Chicago law firm, with a concentration in family law, my sister, Frances Krasnow, guides her clients through some of the most difficult times of their lives—complicated divorces and child custody battles, prenuptial and postnuptial agreements, and same-sex issues ranging from adoptions to marital dissolutions.

Ann Gottschalk Joiner, who went to Camp Fernwood in Maine, helps every faculty and staff member at American University live better. As an executive director in the Office of Human Resources, she oversees employee health and wellness programs, and the coordination of benefits.

Jill Hirschfield helps people hear better, as an audiologist of forty years.

Her younger sister, Agawak alum Carol Hirschfield, helps babies enter the world, as head of a large practice of midwives at Northwestern Memorial Hospital in Chicago. The onetime White Team captain compares the cheerleading she did as the leader of a team to the cheerleading she does in the delivery room.

CAROL

Our impulse toward caregiving comes from the fact that we grow so close to each other in cabin life and in camp life at a young age. We learn compassion and empathy quickly. It's almost as if we live in each other's skin.

I come from a family of three girls. I went to an all-girls' camp. I realized very early the healing power that the sisterhood offers, in my family and among my camp friends.

Pursuing a profession in which I take care of others in emotional and physical ways just evolved naturally. Camp definitely was a factor in my decision to become a midwife, which is all about healing and empowering women throughout the life cycle, from teens to post-menopausal women.

Midwives are nurses, and our whole job is empathy and empowerment, even in the prenatal stage. Women get scared for labor, and we offer reassurance. We tell them: "You are stronger than you know."

How many times did you hear that at camp, from your counselors and your friends? "You are stronger than you know" are words that empower us every day at camp, trying new sports, learning to live on our own.

When patients are in the throes of labor, often I'll literally take them by the face and say: "You've got this!" I remember standing in front of my whole White Team and telling them "We've got this!" I hear from new mothers during their postpartum visits how much my words meant to boost their confidence and strength.

Camp taught me that words matter, actions matter, to do the right thing for each other. We come back from camp different people, nicer people, more patient people, more capable people. We come back as people who put others first.

And some of us lucky ones are invited back as adults, to keep contributing to others at our childhood camps. As director of Raquette Lake Girls Camp, Kim Gutfleish Sklow serves a community of 270 campers and 135 staff members. She was head counselor the summer of 2000, our sons' first camper year and my first year on staff at Raquette Lake Boys Camp. The qualities of responsibility, leadership, and service that fueled her evolution from Raquette Lake camper to director is further demonstrated in her role as a teacher in an all-boys K–9 school in Manhattan.

Kim is fifty-six years young, with a vitality she says stems from "being surrounded by energy and youth, curiosity and excitement, all year round." With this, I could not agree more. Teaching campers and students all four seasons can act as an incomparable pro-aging regimen for us AARP members.

Here is more from Kim on the ways camp shows girls how to take responsibility for themselves and for each other. As she speaks of the growth of campers, she reflects on how she has grown, too.

KIM

Camp raises kids who know how to share, who know how to compromise, who learn to make decisions away from their parents, who learn how to negotiate, who learn how to lead and how to serve others.

My greatest joy is teaching both the campers and counselors these real-life skills. I am teaching girls to feel strong and confident and empowered.

I learned many of these skills as a camper who became more confident and empowered by the older girls and counselors. It was an important awakening to girl power, having grown up with three brothers, one who is my twin.

While childhood has changed from my growing-up

years, with more stress from social media and competition to get into the best schools, my goal is to help every girl understand that she has something to give that will enlighten all of us. And to teach them that we are truly at our best as a community when every light is shining. That is the motto and mantra I communicate on a regular basis at camp.

Encourage others. Empower others. Extinguishing one light makes it that much darker for all of us.

While there is competition in individual sports and team games, the competition that is the most formative at camp is an internal competition to be our best. We teach girls that being our best doesn't mean you have to win. Being our best can mean learning how to rely on each other, to help each other—and to ask for help when you need it.

As I watch the girls grow, I've grown as a leader in so many ways. I've learned to be a better listener. I've learned to be a better collaborator. I've learned to be a much better mediator. You never stop growing at camp.

At the end of every summer I get sweet notes from counselors and campers, that I tack above my desk. They are all different, but the underlying message is the same, thanking me for some moment when a girl felt heard, seen, loved. One reads: "I was having the worst day, and you put your arm around me and walked me down to the lake for swimming."

That's a reminder to me and a reminder I give to the campers: Open your arms and your heart to any girl in need.

I can't tell you how much the open arms and open hearts of girls and women at camp have also helped me become who I am today. My mother died when I was just twenty-two, but she was also a great role model. She taught me that women can, and should, feel empowered to become anything they want to be. I am taking that message forward.

I, too, credit my years as a camper and on staff for an innate desire to teach, serve, and care for others, in raising a family and sculpting a career. When my third and fourth sons were born in one delivery, I left daily journalism and became a freelance writer at home, where I could spend more time with the children.

During that craziest and most inspirational stretch of my life, I wrote my first book, *Surrender-*

ing to Motherhood, a project pieced together during their naps and before sunrise that was four years in the making.

I reflect on those days of holding soft babies, now hard-bodied young men, and what I remember most is that I felt capable. I felt like Carol tells her mothers in labor: "You've got this."

I was trained well at camp.

At the age of sixteen, I was the leader of seventy five girls on the Blue Team. At the age of seventeen, I was responsible for eight ten-year-olds as counselor in Cabin 6. At the age of eighteen, I was in charge of sixteen fifteen-year-olds in Cabin 15.

I was a camp girl. I was a camp counselor. I was used to bedlam. I was used to peacemaking.

I remember soothing our cranky children with the most beautiful of songs that placated us as campers. The boys' favorite was "Let There Be Peace on Earth," with lyrics that go like this:

Let there be peace on earth
And let it begin with me

As I sang it over and over, lying on the carpet between their bedrooms, it generally did bring on sleep and peace.

Rereading this passage from *Surrendering to Motherhood*, I am newly grateful for those fleeting years of their early childhood I got to spend at home.

> *We look at our children, with joy and wonder, but also with a profound sadness, as they change in an eye blink from babies to third-graders to students in colleges too far away. For me, my absolute centering as a human being comes from holding a child in my lap, or slumped over my shoulder. Soon, too soon, these toddlers will be strapping teens who won't sit still for their mother's kisses.*
>
> *Although my generation was reared to crave big careers and worldly pursuits, I have come to realize that true fulfillment and passion, and I'm talking about real passion of the soul, comes not from ascending in the work force but from spending time with*

our families, precious time we can never get back.

The choice to pursue a career as a journalism professor with a flexible schedule was made to put family first. This job I have held for three decades also gives me the opportunity to do what I know how to do best—that is, to teach young people to write well and to be their best selves.

Summers off meant I could play with our children, and later work at their camp. With grown children who now plan their own playdates, it means I get to go back to work at *my* camp.

I watch old camp movies of sports competitions that my father filmed during Parents' Weekend. I am the captain in braids, crouched next to a runner on third base, urging her to steal home, which she does in a cyclone of dust. As the footage continues, I am crouched in front of a heartbroken girl who struck out.

Shortly after, I am standing in front of my somber team, and in a voice thick and hoarse from cheering them on, offering comfort after a really close game that ended in a loss.

If my dad were alive, he would be filming me again, a woman with hair that is now puffs of silver but who still stands in front of campers, like she did when she wore auburn braids.

He would be proud that I am still coaching young girls to be responsible and to know their power—on the field, in their relationships, in making their dreams come true.

Chapter Seven
Tradition

"At sixty-four, I am feeling ageless and free, and grateful that sweet summer is here, that this place is here, that I am here, again and again."

The lake is like glass and the sky is striped with chalky pastels at dusk as the Sunday campfire is about to begin. The smallest girls are lying in the laps of counselors, who are lightly stroking their foreheads and hair. Flushed and teary from smoke and memories, I am seated on a high stool about to present the week's *Agalog* articles.

The setting has changed—Sunday *Agalog* evenings used to be held in the lodge with our camper family of 120 sprawled on the floor. And the reader has changed—it used to be director Oscar in a rocking chair. Now it is me, circled by a camper-counselor population that has ballooned to more than three hundred.

Yet the hush that falls as the articles are shared is the same. There is no laughter. No clapping. The tradition stands.

Sunday is our silent night.

I look out at the girls, and I see me as a child with my head in a lap, serene and stirred by simple words. I see me beaming when my own entry is being read, like this one from a Sunday in 1965 when the theme was Tradition, and I wrote:

> *Agawak is our second home. We have rules we don't love and traditions we love. Like Slo Pokes on movie night. Capture the Flag. Being cared for by every single, solitary person,*

*every single, solitary day. These are a few of
the things that keep us coming back.*

I have revived the *Agalog* themes from decades
past, and Tradition is a popular one. Most of the
articles on this topic address what the writers look
forward to each summer they return, like I voiced
many moons over Blue Lake ago. Most often the
girls choose to spotlight Blue and White games,
signature foods routinely served on certain days,
and reuniting with their friends.

The chef at camp for the past twenty-seven
years is Christopher Domack, who is called
Ducky. The nickname came from high school,
when he tripped in a stairwell, was unharmed,
and laughed so hard he got honky and breathless,
sounding like a duck.

Among Ducky's culinary traditions are: pizzas
on Friday nights, custom-designed by each cabin
group; wings for Wednesday lunches; blueberry
and chocolate-chip pancakes on Sunday mornings; and Saturday cookouts serving up baked
potatoes, and chicken and tofu, barbequed on
the grill.

As Ducky caters to the growing number of vegans and vegetarians, lunches and dinners feature a bountiful salad bar, complete with edamame, broccoli, cauliflower, and beets. Side dishes are locally grown squash and brussels sprouts, roasted with fresh herbs from the camp garden.

In my camper era, with the kitchen run by Chef Mona 'Tutor, our diet was starchy and beefy and artery-clogging. This was way before cholesterol monitoring and research on the evils of gluten— yet we survived. Among Mona's traditional menu items were steak, french fries, and hot fudge sundaes for Saturday lunch, and gooey cinnamon rolls for Sunday breakfasts. For Sunday dinners, we were served greasy baked chicken and mashed potatoes, heaped with butter.

Tofu was definitely not a menu option, nor had I ever heard of it. Vegetables were largely from the can, and our spices were simply salt and pepper.

Mystery meat showed up in many dishes, such as one Mona labeled Slow Boat to China, a tasty stew riddled with water chestnuts that looked like

Gravy Train. Steak at camp was not a tender filet cooked rare. Yet, how we devoured those thin and tough slabs of beef and the heaps of fries slathered in Heinz ketchup.

One dinner, Mona had concocted a soup of fish, potatoes, lima beans, and something green and weedy and indecipherable floating on the top. It was awful, and we held our noses and made snide complaints. Our counselor lit into us immediately, telling us that this meal was more food and better food than a large part of the world's population had ever eaten.

We emptied our bowls of that squishy fish dish.

When I gather with my camp friends, we talk about how the predictability of the menu was one of the traditions we loved most about Agawak. Some women in our circle came from homes where meals consisted of whatever leftovers they could scrounge together from the refrigerator, eaten whenever, and there were no sit-down dinners.

Camp meals were scheduled at the same time every day: breakfast at 8 a.m., lunch at 12:30 p.m., and dinner at 6 p.m., eaten at a big round table.

This cozy circle of laughter and adoration could feel closer than some families of origin.

"It was the only time in my childhood I didn't eat alone," says Marion, a cabinmate from the 1960s. She was an only child to parents who had their gin and tonics while their daughter ate by herself, watching TV.

After every meal, we sang songs, the same songs every summer: sprightly ones at breakfast and lunch, slow and nostalgic ones at dinner. The melodies and lyrics are etched somewhere so deep in our psyches that at fifty, sixty, seventy, and beyond, we can recall every word, and every mood they create.

A popular camp song to rouse us in the morning was "Vim, Vigor, Vitality," which went like this:

Vim, vigor, vitality
Health, happiness, honesty
Words for which we stand,
Living in this happy land
So let's stand together
In fair or stormy weather
Hooray for Agawak!

When we sing this now as women, a song that has been sung by campers since the 1930s, there are plenty of tears when we get to the line *"So let's stand together, in fair or stormy weather."*

In our youth, we could never have imagined just how elongated this pledge to stand together would turn out to be. In that togetherness, then and now, it is, indeed, a very happy land. And when the landscape turns stormy, we are still stuck, tightly, loyally, forever. I am reminded of this today as the text group of twelve alumnae titled Agawak Girls got this sad dispatch from one of us: The cancer is back. Surgery next week.

In a flurry, in less than a minute, there were messages flying to our friend stricken with a returned malignancy:

"Keep up the Agawak spirit."

"You've got to get through this; our camp reunion is coming up soon!"

And this from me: "Just know you are the center of a circle of love, and we are all with you, always."

Our friend calls me, and I say, "WTF." She laughs and says, "I know, WTF." We hang up, and

I look at photos of us together as children, and cannot believe we are this old, though I can believe we are still linked.

It is the nature versus nurture thing; we were raised by different parents at home, but we were raised by the same people and traditions at camp. In this upbringing, camp for some of us had equal or more impact.

Diane Leaf Mehlman was ten when she started at Agawak in 1956, which led to six more years as a camper and seven as a counselor. At the age of seventy, her camp friends form her tightest circle of friends. So filled with vim and vitality were those summers for Diane that she sent her two daughters to Agawak. These girls, now moms in their forties, have daughters that are current campers, an intergenerational legacy that is increasingly common at sleepaway camps.

One of Diane's daughters, Sara Mervis, forty-five, recently joined the Agawak administration team.

Diane remains connected to camp as a board member of the Agawak Alumnae Foundation. She discovered how deeply embedded significant camp traditions are when the board was organizing the camp's ninetieth reunion.

"We were amazed to find out as we talked to women who were campers in the 1930s and 1940s that they had the same experiences we had," says Diane. "We're talking a forty-five-year span of Agawak women, and we all remember running to be first in line to get a Slo Poke on movie night, how we loved the sound of the raindrops on the roofs of our cabins.

"We talked about how the smell of pine trees, wherever we live now, however old we are now, brings us back to the happiest times of our childhood."

I tell Diane that one of my favorite Agawak songs, "No More Saddles, No Levi's," was written during her camp era, in the 1950s. I begin to sing this first stanza over the telephone, and Diane quickly joins in:

No more saddles, no Levi's
No more cooking outdoors with the flies
No more pack trips, no steak fries
Kiss the camp goodbye.

Well, I never did have to kiss the camp good-bye, and I still wear my old Levi's on pack trips with the girls. These songs are markers of each passage that has led to the present; they are the soundtracks of my whole life.

We sang them as fourth graders. We sang them as teenagers. We sang them as mothers to our children, who sing them to their children. We sing them whenever we are together. We sing them when we are apart, over telephone lines. I am teaching these songs to the next generation of camp girls.

These foods and these songs and these traditions are the fixed picture frames that shelter the fluidity of our lives as they progress. We are forever buttressed by the camp rituals that provided structure and stability in our young lives.

On Saturday mornings, in an activity called Scrub, we washed our hair and bodies in Blue Lake, with the Prell shampoo and Ivory soap we bought at the camp canteen. Bathing is now only done in the shower houses, eliminating soapy pollutants from dirtying the lake. On Sunday mornings, we wrote letters on the waterfront lawn, as classical music played on a record player through speakers.

Wednesdays were cookout nights, and each cabin group retreated to a designated lakeside spot to blacken our hot dogs to salty crispiness.

At 9 p.m., "Taps" was played on a bugle, signaling time for flashlights out and whispers only for all but the oldest campers, who could talk until 10 p.m. That window of time when we were the big girls who could stay up an hour longer is an ingrained teenage memory.

In chenille bathrobes and fuzzy slippers, we gossiped about first kisses and second base, and heartache with first loves, while painting each other's nails, braiding each other's hair.

There was no morning confusion on what to wear as we all dressed in the same clothes. Agawak was then strictly a uniform camp: navy bottoms and powder-blue collared shirts by day, white-collared shirts and navy bottoms at night, white bottoms and white-collared shirts on Sundays. No T-shirts, no jeans, no two-piece bathing suits, no other colors.

We wore navy tank suits with colored rubber swim caps that marked our swimming skills, going from white, green, and blue to red, yellow, and purple.

Traditions that endure, and defined daily schedules, are central components of most summer camps. A predictable schedule and routine gave us a great sense of security, particularly girls whose home schedules were not so set and secure.

"Camp was a place that was completely reliable, and this was really a big deal for me," says Ann Gottschalk Joiner, the alumna of Camp Fernwood. "My parents divorced when I was seven, and when I was ten my mother got remarried to a man who was my ideal dad. It was crushing when my stepfather died a few years later. The structure of camp was a comforting escape from a topsy-turvy home life. I knew that every summer was going to be exactly the same—the same activities, the same traditions. Camp was more home for me than my real home."

While uniforms are still required at many traditional camps, like Fernwood and Raquette Lake, the mandatory dress code at Agawak lasted only until the early 1980s. Today, anything goes.

It is common to see girls come to meals in yoga

pants and drapey tank tops that fall off the shoulder to reveal sports bras. Tutus appear often, too. The girls' palette for their fashion choices seems to be every shade but the camp colors, though white shirts and navy bottoms are required on Sundays.

When I see the girls arrive for swimming in neon-pink string bikinis, I imagine our late waterfront director, Beaver, blowing her whistle that was always around her neck, angrily rounding them up and making them change.

As a witness to the transformation of our camp culture, I admit that I miss the days when we were unified in uniforms. I miss seeing a battalion dressed alike during the serious ritual of raising a flag. I love that many pillars of our camp structure remain, and those regimens offer the comforting escape that Ann Gottschalk Joiner found.

Some in this generation of campers have the topsy-turvy home lives she spoke of; all of them are coming of age in a topsy-turvy world. They can count on camp for its order and predictability.

Perhaps the most crucial Agawak mainstay: Once a member of the Blue Team or White Team, always a Blue or White. Many team cheers are the same as campers chanted during World War II and the Great Depression.

And another abiding given: The girls love camp as much as we did.

Agawak lifer Olivia Baker, the former Blue Team captain, values the impact of tradition and rituals as much as we did in our era. Sitting on a bench that has been on the lip of Blue Lake since my camper years, we talk about the impact of rules and routines.

OLIVIA

Our camp is so much about these rituals that, even at my age, I have come to appreciate the importance of tradition. I like the way things work in a systematic way, repeated year after year. At camp, there is a soothing rhythm to our lives. Like the seasons, you know what to expect and when to expect it.

Capture the Flag, boating and swimming meets, always are played the same weeks each camp season. During the sixth week of camp, the oldest girls still go on a canoe trip through the Boundary Waters near Canada. Blue Lake is still clean and cold. We still eat a lot, even though we swear we're on diets. Campers and counselors still sob as the buses pull out of Agawak on the last day. And we all come back for as long as we can.

As a freshman in college, what Olivia has yet to realize is how a childhood spent in a community of traditions can foster the ability to build a stronger family.

I was certainly not the perfect mother, but when our four grown sons reflect on their childhood, they say one of the best things I did was to be reliable. They had a consistent schedule at home, and like Olivia appreciates about Agawak, knew what to expect and when to expect it. There was a rhythm to their days and years.

We have been vacationing in the same Delaware beach house on the Atlantic Ocean since our oldest son was born thirty years ago. I am still with the same husband I married thirty-three years ago. I have worked as a professor at the same university for thirty years.

Our kids attended the same school from prekindergarten through high school graduation.

They grew from babies to young men in the same house. They still live a short car or train ride away, and return for the holidays that happen at the same time every year. I serve the same brisket and noodle kugel that my mother made, and that her mother made.

I am about to spend my seventeenth summer at Camp Agawak.

I was born the day my parents bought our house in Oak Park, Illinois, and I lived there until I went to college. My parents were married for thirty-four years until death did they part, with the passing of my father.

Growing up, my mother served breakfast at 7 a.m., lunch at noon, and dinner at 5:30 p.m. I raised our sons on an identical schedule, only they ate their lunches at school. On those brown paper bags that I filled with a sandwich, a yogurt, a fruit, and two cookies, I always drew a big red heart around their names, spelled out with black marker.

Deep roots and rituals provide a safe harbor in a shaky and unpredictable world. I have traveled to many majestic destinations, with lots of spectacular views. My favorite views to wake up to are the Severn River and Blue Lake.

I am a different animal than many of my journalism colleagues who prefer the nomadic life, shifting posts and publications in different cities and countries every few years. I work my best and feel my best when operating with people, and from places, that hold my history.

At our last alumni reunion, we talked about how we are dealing with aging, covering subjects that ranged from staying married to getting divorced to loosening flesh. I relayed that at my sixtieth birthday, I noticed changes happening: A slight jiggle with a lift of the arm, even though I lift weights. Droops around the mouth. Sore hips. An awakening, troubling and true, that fine facial lines are now grooves and that my hands, with their bulging veins and spots, look more like my mother's hands.

Throughout it all, the rhythm of camp and our friendships is steady and sure. What a blessing to still have this shatterproof bastion of youth that creates everlasting hope and a spring to our step.

Camp girls keep us centered and optimistic.

I am ageless when I wear the blue plaid flannel shirt my mom bought at Sears for the 1963 camp season. I would rather be wearing that shirt and my navy sweatpants from the summer of 1968 than black high heels and a $400 little black dress.

I hope I last as long as Agawak has, though camp is clearly adding years to my life span. Gerontologists that study centenarians tell us there are three major factors that contribute to successful aging: remaining productive and engaged with work; staying fit; and sustaining intimate relationships.

On all three fronts, camp is a fountain of youth. I love my job. I get lots of physical activity. I get an abundance of emotional support from my oldest friends.

Camp has even boosted my marriage.

My father told me decades ago that the ticket to survival is to "swing with it," to swing through obstacles, knowing better days are ahead. So far, my spouse and I have swung with mounting bills, unruly teenagers, the death of both sets of parents, and the spells of loneliness that accompany our empty nest.

I attribute much of our staying power to taking breaks from each other. Lots of my long-partnered friends swear by separate vacations. I swear by separate summers. I go to camp and Chuck stays home, content to be working as long as he wants, watching sports as long as he wants, doing whatever the hell he wants for as long as he wants.

When we grow on our own, we are able to best grow together. And we have infallible trust.

Chuck is a sculptor as well as an architect and a woodworker. One of his prize projects was designing our new synagogue after a snowstorm caused the roof of the old building to collapse. One summer, I returned from camp and there was a ten-foot, six-hundred-pound sculpture lying on a large plywood stand in our living room. It depicted Miriam and Aaron and the other Israelites from Exodus walking through the parting seas toward Mount Sinai. Clumps of clay covered the floor.

His chiseled rendition of Exodus is now the breathtaking door of the temple ark, which holds the Torah. His masterpiece was created during eighteen-hour days, lasting until 3 and 4 a.m., during the weeks I was gone. This schedule would never have been possible if I had been home nagging him to stop the pounding and to turn down the guitar music of John Renbourn, which he likes to play loudly.

The independence and self-reliance that become part of a camp girl's DNA come up in our alumni conversations about marriages that failed due to partners who stifled personal growth.

I have learned from the books I have written about relationships that the happiest couples have their own passions and pursuits outside of their partnerships. I know from my own marriage that summer camp makes me more interesting and fulfilled, as do Chuck's separate summers.

We come together more grateful for each other, more romantic, and less annoyed by each other's annoying habits. He is a camper, too, after all, strong and capable on his own.

Anna Rothman, the founder of Camp Wicosuta in Hebron, New Hampshire, must have also felt that the old adage is true: "Absence makes the heart grow fonder." Her great-granddaughter Anne Rothman told me this of the Wicosuta matriarch, a woman who started the camp in 1920, owned the camp for twenty-five years, and died at the age of eighty-eight in 1974.

"My great-grandmother was a pioneer in so many ways," says Anne. "What Jewish lady in 1920 is going to go build a camp in the middle of nowhere? During all those years she owned Wicosuta, my great-grandfather only came up to camp once. He didn't help her run it. He didn't help her pay for it. It was her endeavor. And it was a really big deal to have a marriage like this during her times."

The couple stayed married for nearly fifty years.

Anne considers Wicosuta "the backbone of my life," a camp she attended, as did her grandmother, mother, sister, and a dozen other relatives.

As parents, the life skills rooted in our childhoods spent romping in the woods have a weighted effect on how we raise our own children. We are intentional in constructing an environment that fosters open-mindedness and courage, creativity and tradition.

From the time my sons were toddlers, we set out to turn them into campers, who would be comfortable in nature, and with all sorts of people. While my family's body of water is the Severn River and not Blue Lake, and our Maryland trees are not as towering as those in Wisconsin, we have carved out a life that has felt like camp.

Our boys grew up kayaking on the river, sleeping in tents on our hill, cooking s'mores over our firepit, drinking beer with their friends at that firepit when Mom and Dad were not home.

I am writing this at 11 p.m. after spending hours at that firepit with all four sons and my husband. The boys came home to celebrate Mother's Day weekend. Zane fed the fire with wood he chopped. Isaac whittled points on sticks with his Swiss Army knife to spear marshmallows. Theo did the beverage runs to the kitchen, keeping cold drinks in our hands. Jack played the guitar. Isaac sat back, eyes closed, content, at peace.

They asked me to lead them in a medley of camp songs I began singing to them as lullabies when they were babies. I start off with their favorite, "Peace I Ask of Thee, Oh River." They joined in as I sang in a wine-laced voice, slightly off-key, as Jack strummed along. The song starts out *"Peace I ask of thee, oh river, peace, peace, peace. When I learn to live serenely, cares will cease."*

My cares have not totally ceased in the twenty-eight years since we fled city life to a house on the river, though many stressors have diminished. My kids grew up learning what their parents learned—that nature slows us down and accelerates self-exploration. Here, we can find pockets of peace in every day, on a secluded patch of grass, under a tree.

Camper kids with camper moms pitched tents together and slept in their backyards. We are the moms that split up our children's friends into two teams and built birthday parties around Capture the Flag.

We are the moms who snapped open the shades and woke our children with this tune from *Oklahoma*, often sung at camp breakfasts: *"Oh, what a beautiful morning, oh, what a beautiful day. I've got a beautiful feeling. Everything's going my way."*

We are women who learned early on that it is up to us to make things go our own way, with focus and hard work. We want our kids to know the same.

Two of our sons now lead hiking and canoe trips for younger children. One spends part of his summer at Agawak teaching tennis and camping skills.

When they were young children themselves before their sleepaway years, I ran a family day camp on the woodsy grounds of our Maryland home. Most days, several of their friends would join in. I wrote out a schedule of five activities every day, patterned after our routine at Agawak—though activities were more like Hike To The Park and Help Mom Wash Her Car.

I have kept all the schedules in hopes that someday our sons will run their own backyard Camp Anthonys, gearing up their kids for the next step of sleepaway summers. My husband's last name is Anthony.

I am thinking of all of this—the circle of my life through childhood and child-rearing—as I start another camp season. I am imagining the beckoning lake, where I will instinctively glide into the breaststroke with a frog kick I learned fifty-four years ago. I am feeling ageless and free, and grateful that sweet summer is here, that this place is here, that I am here, again and again.

Blue Lake has been my companion for longer than most people I know. On that water in a kayak, or in that water doing laps, I find answers for whatever is boggling me come quicker, with more clarity, unfailingly.

Back from my first swim of the new camp season, I am sitting in a wet bathing suit wrapped in a towel, looking out my cabin window at trees turned translucent green from the early morning sun. The campers are asleep and the only sounds are muffled steps from the tiny feet of two black squirrels.

Talk of traditional foods and summer camp schedules may seem insignificant in the face of the woes of the world. Yet it is the power of these ordinary and restorative routines that even out the rest of our lives.

My friends who never went to camp also romance the soul of summer as the season that thrusts us all into an open-ended sense of time and expanded self-awareness. We all revel in the sun and the added opportunity for more outdoor play, and more time with our families.

We all know that the woods and the water pose a much-needed escape from the mad whirl of our lives, that frenzy of commitments that cram our calendars once fall rolls around.

When camp is over and my own calendar gets crammed, I count on the calm of the Severn River. I have gazed at the river while feeding squealing babies, and I watch that water now as a mother with a quiet nest.

The solace of the sea is a source for present joy and for remembering.

I am looking at footage of camp movies from 1965: I am thick and tall, in a navy-blue tank suit and pigtails. My mother is clutching my waist, and the lake is in the background. I am hearing her voice today, exactly as it sounded on that Saturday afternoon of Parents' Weekend fifty-five years ago. She is telling me how proud she is of me that I know how to slalom water-ski, and that I scored a home run for the Blue Team in an earlier kickball game.

My friends remember how loudly she yelled at team games, amid the crowd of more restrained, self-conscious parents. I remember how much she loved how much I loved camp.

As I keep watching the footage, I am remembering how much I loved my parents, and how their love for me becomes newly, fully alive in these priceless family films.

The sequence of this film ends with a shot of the backs of my mom, me, and my sister, Frances, our arms around each other. We are walking slowly to my parents' silver Tornado, signifying the end of Parents' Weekend.

I turn around and smile broadly at the camera, waving and flashing a mouthful of braces.

When our parents pulled away, my sister and I would stand there for a while, feeling sad and drained. That would last for five minutes at most, before we rushed back to our cabins, to other girls in pigtails and braces and swimsuits still wet from showing off for their own moms and dads.

These are the girls with whom we would reunite every June, and grow together—as our braces came off, our pigtails were cut into the flip that Sally

Field wore in the *Gidget* TV show, then grown into the longer locks of then–top model Cheryl Tiegs, who (and this really dates us) is now seventy-one.

We huddled together through stormy waters on weeklong canoe trips, and are huddled together on this cold night in Cabin 12 during our reunion, a cabin that most of us slept in as girls.

The next morning, we will swim in the same lake where we earned our colored caps, the same seaweed tickling our legs. We will tease the frogs leaping around the shorelines, descendants of the frogs we used to catch together as kids.

Acknowledgments

First off, I would like to thank my editor at Hachette, Gretchen Young, for her meticulous attention to every word. Guided by her sharp insights and gentle hand, Gretchen helped me excavate the most detailed memories of the camp girl I was then and fresh impressions of the camp girl I am now. Because of her caring leadership, I was able to weave the past and the present into one book that is wholly about love.

Gretchen did not go to summer camp, though

she attended an all-girls high school and understood the central message of *Camp Girls* from the start: that it is our girlfriends that keep us grounded and growing and entertained. I am proud to call Gretchen not only my editor, but also a really smart new friend.

I am hugely grateful to my next-door neighbors Gail and Stan Watkins, who allowed me to occupy a cozy den in their home, daily, for months, as my "writer's cove." In this room on the Severn River, spare and silent, I was able to access the most minute and precise imagery, with only my memories as company. Though we have the same river view, I wrote my best at their home, detached from my cell phone and refrigerator.

I spoke to Liz Weinstein, one of my camp besties, at least once a day, over the years I was imagining, then composing, this book. We talked on the phone while we were on separate walks in separate states, while we were having a glass of wine in our separate kitchens. We talked any time I needed a team game or cabin prank refreshed to spill onto my pages. It was Liz, a graphic designer, who helped me relaunch our camp magazine,

Agalog, after it had been gone for thirty-some years. I could not have done this without Liz by my virtual side—her in Illinois, me in Maryland.

Another camp sister, Margie Gordon, deserves so much gratitude. For a long weekend each summer, several of our cabinmates from the 1960s and 1970s go up to Agawak for an alumni reunion. Margie loved being back so much that she went to work at camp the following summer, teaching yoga and leading overnight trips. What a gift to be approaching Medicare age and to be together as camp girls again.

Thank you to all our camp girls, many now grandmothers, who have come back to camp for our July reunions. As our iconic camp song "I'm Strong for Camp Agawak" goes, *"No matter the weather, we will all stick together,"* and we have clearly done that. We braved thunderstorms on canoe trips in Canada as children. As adults, we are braving illness and the loss of parents and siblings. Surrounding by this girl circle, I always feel hopeful and youthful and wildly alive.

So here's to our aging, ageless Agawak tribe: Peggy Gilbert, Karen Schwartz Sutker, Terry

Worth Sigman, Margie Worth, Jill Meltzer, Carol Hirschfield, Toni Chaikin, Laurie Holleb Klapman, Lori Gilford, Karen Feldman Edelstein, and Susan Wiedenbeck. They pay to stay, with donations to the Agawak Alumnae Foundation, which provides camper scholarship funds.

Terry Schwartz, my closest friend during our camp years, is not able to join us for these reunions. But our FaceTime and phone chats have made my life so much richer. I love you, Terry. You are always teaching me something.

Another huge nod of appreciation goes to Kathi and Eddie Lapidus, owners of Raquette Lake Camps, for boys and girls. They welcomed me as a staff member when our four sons attended their camp. I spoke to Kathi while researching this book, and we shared our enduring commitment to working with young children and teens.

As she puts it: "I love watching the self-esteem it gives campers, no matter who they are. Some might be great at songwriting, some may be great at dancing, some at soccer, some in the water. Camp is an opportunity for everyone to shine at something." Kathi and Eddie gave me the opportunity to shine at something I loved deeply and had left behind, living in a camp community. This is a central part of me that I came to realize I must never lose again.

Enter Mary Fried, owner/director of Camp Agawak, who made it possible to remain at camp. I met Mary at our ninetieth reunion, and she invited me to come back the following summer to direct a writing program and resurrect the camp magazine that had died in the early 1980s. That first summer will turn into my seventh summer when I head to camp again in June of 2020.

What a gift Mary has given me. I got my literary start writing for *Agalog* at the age of eight, in 1963. My whole girlhood streams through me as I watch the children feel what I felt, how the words pour forth as the heart opens up under an open sky, in the hush of nature. This writer is without enough words to express just how very deeply thankful I am to Mary, for getting me back to Agawak.

And thank you to her husband, Bill Fuhrmann, the camp waterskiing director who serves as our Director of Fun when the alumni camp girls visit, taking us waterskiing and on long pontoon rides around our cherished Blue Lake.

Another thank-you goes to Mary's brother-in-law Mike Fried. When I started this book three years ago, Mike connected me with key contacts in the camping industry that served as critical sources. Many of our awesome international Agawak staff members come to us through Mike's work as vice president, camp counselor program, for Camp Counselor USA.

The camp associate director, Chris Garcia, is deserving of my unending gratitude. Chris is my go-to person at Agawak, for everything from getting me supplies for our writing activity to being my swimming partner to giving me answers on any camp question that comes up. She knows it all!

Though it was the pine forest of northern Wisconsin that intensified my passion for writing, it was my sister, Frances, who gave me the confidence to keep at it. We were campers together, and when my articles were read at the Sunday *Agalog* nights, she would always hug me and say, "You are such a good writer." In college, I majored in photojournalism and was veering toward pursuing photography over writing as a career. Frances said to me, "You can take photos to go with your articles. You can't give up your writing."

Thank you, to the woman I call Sis, for keeping me on track. You believed in me as a child, and having your love and support throughout our long life together has always helped me believe in myself. I love you so much. And to my brother, Greg, you are the best at making me laugh and relax, which was so appreciated during the many months of hard thinking and writing.

In this book that stems from my own empowering experiences in camping, I branched out into research on the universal impact of sleepaway summers on the formation of successful adulthoods. Leaders at the American Camp Association provided me with layers of historical and statistical data. I am so thankful particularly for the generosity and expertise of three ACA leaders, who answered my many queries, during interviews on the phone and in person: Tom Rosenberg, president/CEO of the ACA; Harriet Lowe, the longtime editor in chief of *Camping Magazine*; and Laurie Browne, director of research.

My literary agent, Gail Ross, has been encouraging me to write a book about summer camp ever since we began working together some two decades ago. Here it is, Gail, because of you. I give you an enormous thank-you, my irrepressible agent and dear friend who never fails to get me to write what I was meant to write.

May our journey together continue to be fruitful—and long.

To my husband, Chuck, and our four sons, thank you for listening to my camp stories and to my camp songs all of these years. I love you so, so much. I have watched you boys, former camp kids, turn into young men who know how to deal in the woods, and in life.

And, Chuck, not every spouse would approve of a wife who spends summers at her old camp. You make my dreams come true. I know you think that camp is my everything. Camp is my most things; it is you and the kids who are my everything. To Chuck, my steadfast husband of thirty-three years, I thank you for supporting my pursuit of endless camp adventures. You help me become a writer and mother and wife who feels like she has it all!

Finally, I end with the most important thank-you of all, to my departed parents, Helene and Theodore Krasnow, creators of this camp girl. You sent me to Agawak at the end of third grade. I still go to camp more than a half century later. You were my first loves, and though you are not here anymore, you gave me so many lasting loves: for nature, for sports, for my camp-girl circle, for tradition.

Wherever you are, Mom and Dad, I know you are with me, cheering me on like you did when you watched me in the heat of Blue and White Team competition.

About the Author

Iris Krasnow is a *New York Times* best-selling author, as well as a professor and camp counselor. During the school year, she teaches writing and gender studies at American University, and she spends summers at Camp Agawak. She has written *Surrendering to Motherhood*, *Surrendering to Marriage*, *Surrendering to Yourself*, *I Am My Mother's Daughter*, *The Secret Lives of Wives*, and *Sex After...* Iris is a regular contributor to AARP publications, a columnist for the Pulitzer Prize–winning *Annapolis Capital Gazette*, and a frequent keynote speaker who gave a popular TEDx talk on relationships. She has been featured on *Oprah*, *The Today Show*, *All Things Considered*, *Good Morning America*, and CNN.